Contents

When We're 65

Reforming Canada's Retirement Income System

John B. Burbidge, James Cutt,
Paul Dickinson, Newman Lam,
Michael J. Prince, Christopher Ragan,
and William B.P. Robson

The Social
Policy Challenge 13

John Richards
and
William G. Watson,
Series Co-Editors

C.D. Howe Institute

C.D. Howe Institute publications are available from:
Renouf Publishing Company Limited, 5369 Canotek Road, Unit 1,
Ottawa, Ontario K1J 9J3; tel.: 613-745-2665; fax: 613-745-7660

and from Renouf's stores at:
71½ Sparks Street, Ottawa; phone (613) 238-8985
12 Adelaide Street West, Toronto; phone (416) 363-3171

For trade book orders, please contact:
McGraw-Hill Ryerson Limited, 300 Water Street,
Whitby, Ontario L1N 9B6; phone (416) 430-5050

Institute publications are also available in microform from:
Micromedia Limited, 20 Victoria Street,
Toronto, Ontario M5C 2N8

This book is printed on recycled, acid-free paper.

Canadian Cataloguing in Publication Data

Main entry under title :
When we're 65 : reforming Canada's retirement income system

(The social policy challenge ; 13)
Includes bibliographical references.
ISBN 0-88806-359-8

1. Canada Pension Plan.   2. Old age pensions – Canada.
3. Retirement income – Canada. I. Burbidge, John,
1948–   . II. C.D. Howe Institute. III. Series.

HD7129.W46 1996   368.4′3′00971   C96-932232-1

Cover design by Leroux Design Inc.
Printed in Canada by Kromar Printing Ltd.,
Winnipeg, Manitoba, December 1996.

Foreword

This volume is the thirteenth in the C.D. Howe Institute's "The Social Policy Challenge," one of the most ambitious series of publications in its history. The 15 studies in the series range from workfare to pensions, from unemployment insurance (UI) to workers' compensation, from housing to aboriginal concerns.

The publication of this series is a daunting task not just for its scope, but also for the urgency and importance of the issues it addresses. Canada needs to modernize its basic social programs — programs that were conceived in an era of rapid economic growth and expanding benefits for the recipients of ever-multiplying public services.

Like many other Canadians, I believe the time is right for a wholesale re-examination of this country's social policies, for several reasons.

First, Canada's fiscal situation remains deeply unsatisfactory, with the cost of servicing accumulated debt continuing to drive taxes up, and ongoing government borrowing cutting into an already low private sector saving rate. Expenditures on social programs are such an important part of public spending that ongoing re-evaluation of the effectiveness of such programs and resolution in ending those that do not measure up must be part of the solution.

Second, Canada is at a crossroads. The phrase is, of course, a rhetorician's reflex. Hardly a year goes by without someone's publishing a volume with that title. And to some extent the cliché is always appropriate: modern democracies make policy decisions almost daily, so they are continually at a crossroads. Still, 1997 will see further changes to federal-provincial transfers — and possibly the taxing powers of the two levels of government as well. Everything is on the table for discussion. No doubt a consensus is developing that Canada has hit the ceiling when it comes to taxes. Even Canadians of the middle-of-the-road variety are no longer willing to finance the apparently unending expansion of the welfare state into more and more marginal activities.

Third, there is increasing concern that many of the programs Canadian governments have put in place over the years may not be good for the people they are supposed to help. Within the academic community, it is now respectable to speak of "transfer dependency," a concept for which economist Thomas Courchene was widely criticized when he introduced it into the Canadian debate in the 1970s. Politicians and commentators across the ideological spectrum now agree that policies that were introduced for very good short-term reasons have created harmful long-term incentives. For example, many Canadians have changed their lifestyles to conform to the rules of the UI and welfare systems. As the growth of Ontario's welfare caseload in the early 1990s illustrated, transfer dependency may no longer be a problem exclusive to the Atlantic region.

Canadians and their governments thus are likely to be preoccupied with social policy over the next few years. It was with this in mind that the C.D. Howe Institute decided to undertake this in-depth examination of social programs. In choosing the co-editors of the series — John Richards, Associate Professor of Business Administration at Simon Fraser University, and William Watson, Associate Professor of Economics, McGill University — I sought to bring a balance of views to the Institute's work. John Richards was a member of Allan Blakeney's New Democratic government in Saskatchewan in the early 1970s. William Watson terms himself "a member of that beleaguered cultural minority, the Canadian right." Although both are experts in the field of economics, neither had previously concentrated his formidable energies in the social policy area, and I felt they would bring a fresh view to some of the same old policy conundrums.

Readers will note that each volume in the series contains differing, at times opposing, views as to whether a particular social program works as intended, needs fixing, or should be left alone. If the conclusion is that a program does need modernizing, the authors will recommend necessary reforms and ways to bring them about.

The C.D. Howe Institute's aim in presenting this series is to raise the level of public debate on issues of national interest by presenting diverse points of view — whether or not it agrees with them — in publications that are well researched and well grounded. The Institute hopes that, in so doing, it will give Canadians much to think about, including the information they require to exercise their responsibilities as citizens.

This volume was copy edited by Deborah Caruso, Lenore d'Anjou, Anthony Luengo, and Barry A. Norris, and prepared for publication by Wendy Longsworth. The analysis and opinions presented in the study are the responsibility of the authors and do not necessarily reflect the views of the Institute's members or Board of Directors.

Thomas E. Kierans
President and
Chief Executive Officer

The Study in Brief

Canadians celebrated the end of World War II in the most wholesome and optimistic way possible, by procreating prolifically. In 1944, 294,000 children were born in Canada. But in 1945, 1946, and 1947, births totaled 301,000, 344,000, and 373,000, respectively. And the baby binge continued, passing 400,000 in 1952 and reaching an all-time high of 479,275 in 1959. By contrast, in 1994 only 386,350 new Canadians were born, even though the country's overall population was 2.4 times what it had been in 1946 and 1.7 times what it had been in 1959. Because the unprecedented baby boom was followed by an almost unprecedented baby bust — birth rates were only marginally higher in the 1970s and 1980s than during the Great Depression — Canada's baby boomers celebrated the fiftieth anniversary of the end of World War II and their own looming half-centuries much less optimistically, by worrying about how they would finance their retirements, if in fact they could afford to retire.

In theory, the pension problem is simple. Assuming the boomers *are* able to retire, some way has to be found to give them a share of whatever economic output Canadian society produces in the years after 2010, when they turn 65. One way is for them to acquire their own legal title to future output — that is, to save. They can save either entirely on their own, out of after-tax dollars, or with the help of their fellow taxpayers, in tax-assisted vehicles such as Registered Pension Plans (RPPs) or Registered Retirement Savings Plans (RRSPs). A second way in which they can provide for their future income is, in effect, to depend on the kindness of strangers and hope that younger Canadians will give them a share of whatever they may be earning in the years following 2010. This is not so unlikely a possibility as it may sound. Canadians have been sharing in this way since 1907, when the country's first public pensions were introduced (a year, it should be noted, after the first *parliamentary* pensions came into being: political charity has always begun at home in this country). An obvious disadvantage of this type of "pay-as-you-go" or "pay-go" scheme is that, when there are relatively few payers compared with the number of would-be retirees, the payers may decide they do not want to pay the very high premiums — taxes, really — necessary to finance the standard of living to which retirees would like to grow accustomed. On the other hand, they may not withdraw their generosity entirely for, in a chain-link version of Christianity's golden rule, they may wish to be treated in their old age the same way they treated the generation before them.

Ethics aside, there is also the problem of which of these two schemes — saving or sharing — will cause 2010's economic output to be greater. The US economist Martin Feldstein, Chairman of Ronald Reagan's Council of Economic Advisers, has written extensively on the possibility that the existence of pay-go savings plans may reduce future wealth by encouraging people to save less, thus reducing the future stock of real capital. His latest estimate is that Social Security reduces private saving in the United States by almost 60 percent, which obviously could have a large effect on future economic output (Feldstein 1996). If Social Security will finance my retirement, people may think, I only need to save enough to top it up. If this kind of thinking causes them to save less, the country's capital stock will not grow as much as it otherwise would. But if the future capital stock is smaller, future economic output will be lower, since capital accumulation is a major source of increased productivity. Of course, this kind of thinking may become less and less common as more and more people come to believe that Social Security — or in our case, the Canada and Quebec Pension Plans (CPP/QPP) — will not provide much, if any payoff in retirement.

How best to handle the retirement problem is obviously a fascinating mix of morality, politics, and the theory of economic growth, and it becomes ever more compelling as, for many of us, retirement moves closer to the middle of the radar screen. This thirteenth volume of the C.D. Howe Institute's "The Social Policy Challenge" includes five papers on different aspects of the retirement challenge. The volume opens with two papers presenting very specific policy proposals — one that CPP funding be stepped up sharply and then gradually phased out in favor of a privatized plan, and the other that RRSPs be replaced by a more general form of consumption tax. The book closes with three papers that, in effect, provide background to the pensions debate. The first looks at the economic theory of transfers between generations, the second examines the effects of demographic changes on the CPP, and the third discusses what the author regards as six common misperceptions about the CPP.

William Robson:
Fix the CPP, Then Phase It Out

The book opens with a paper bearing the provocative title of "Ponzi's Pawns," written by William Robson, a Senior Policy Analyst at the C. D. Howe Institute. As Robson explains, Charles Ponzi (1882?–1949) was a particularly audacious practitioner of what came to be known as the "Ponzi scheme" or the "pyramid scheme" — a scam under which contributions paid in by new members finance dividends to existing members. In a Ponzi scheme, as Gertrude Stein said of Oakland, California, there is "no there there": no real investment underlies the scheme. If the number of new contributors does not continue to grow, dividends dry up and the scheme collapses. Robson argues this is precisely the danger faced by the Canada Pension Plan.

The CPP is not *exactly* a Ponzi scheme, of course. Ponzi went to jail for his plan because he represented to investors that there *was* a there there, that he was actually taking their money and investing in postal-reply coupons, which, to begin with at least, he had in fact been doing. The CPP, by contrast, is perfectly transparent, even if most Canadians are not familiar with its details. Moreover, it has at least a small there there: by law, it must maintain a small capital fund sufficient to pay out two years of benefits in case the payroll taxes that finance it suffer a cyclical decline. When people talk about the CPP "going bust," they are referring to the possibility that, as current payouts to pensioners begin to exceed current contributions by wage earners, this rainy day fund will be depleted. In fact, unless payouts or payroll taxes are adjusted, that is almost certain to happen early in the next century, but that does not mean the plan will have "gone bust." Quite the contrary, it will collapse only if future wage earners decide they no longer wish to contribute. Because official projections indicate that, as the ratio of pensioners to wage earners rises over the next few decades contribution rates will have to rise as high as 14 or 15 percent in order to maintain payouts, Robson believes that more and more wage earners probably will become "reluctant players" and vote for political parties that promise to reduce their contribution rates. The danger is compounded by current politicians' habit of making "soothing but misleading statements" (p. 31) about the importance of maintaining payouts to current beneficiaries, who naturally are upset by talk about one of their principal sources of retirement income "going bust."

At the heart of Robson's paper are calculations showing how young Canadians are likely to fare under the CPP. The chief actuary of Canada has estimated that, for people who reached retirement age in 1976, the CPP paid off at an effective annual return of more than 30 percent on their contributions; "[b]y contrast, average participants born in 1988 are expected to receive a return about one-sixth as high — 5.2 percent, which is barely more than 1.5 percent after allowing for projected inflation" (p. 35). Another way to look at this problem is to see how much worse off young Canadians would be under the CPP compared with how they could fare by contributing to a fully funded plan — that is, one that invested in assets such as stocks, bonds, mortgages, and so on. Assuming the return to money invested in such assets averaged 2.5 percent in real terms, Robson calculates that today's ten-year-olds who earned the CPP's maximum pensionable earnings (currently $35,000) over their working lives would be worse off by just over a year's earnings under the pay-go CPP, compared with what would have been available under a funded plan. Anyone born today would be worse off by a year and a half's earnings. If real returns were 4.5 percent instead of 2.5 percent, however, "[t]he representative [CPP] participant who is ten years old today stands to lose the equivalent of five and a half years of covered earnings at age 65 by participating in an unreformed CPP," while today's and tomorrow's toddlers would be six to six and a half years worse off (p. 41).

Robson calls this way of doing things "embarrassing" and "unconscionable." He also doubts it is sustainable. It currently appears to be: "most voters have already seen some of their funds disappear into the scheme and have therefore begun to develop an interest in preserving it long enough to get their benefits" (p. 42). The problem is that, while ten-year-olds and toddlers do not vote, 50- and 60-year-olds do. If the system were wound up in five years' time, with benefits continuing to be paid only to people who were already receiving them at that time, people who had contributed for 20 or 30 years would be big losers. Even though the gain to younger Canadians would exceed their loss, Robson calculates that more voters would be opposed to a windup than would favor it, which means it probably would not pass. In another ten years, however, the political balance begins to change: more young Canadians will reach voting age, while more older Canadians will already be receiving benefits and therefore would be unaffected by a windup. Sometime between 2011 and 2021, Robson reckons, the political balance will tip in favor of winding up the plan — although, of course, there may be an element of self-fulfilling prophecy in all this: once Canadians understand the balance eventually will tip toward a windup, "the increasing sense that money put into the plan was money thrown away would prompt demands for a quicker windup" (p. 47). Robson concludes that, "[o]n balance, those politicians who promise to overturn an unreformed CPP — and there will be many of them in the twenty-first century — will likely get an increasingly enthusiastic response" (p. 48).

What to do? Robson provides options both for the reform of the CPP and for its replacement. Phasing in much higher rates — a maximum rate of, say, 11.9 percent rather than the 9.5 percent rate currently projected in ten years' time — with a consequent buildup in the retirement fund, would force all current contributors to pay more of their own retirement, which would relieve part of the future burden on young people. If CPP benefits were scaled back by 10 percent over a ten-year period, this would also lighten the load on future contributors. The penalty they would face compared with what they could earn in a fully funded plan would fall to a little less than four and a half years' earnings, which is clearly better than the six to six and a half years' earnings the status quo costs them. Robson calculates that after these reforms the day when a majority of Canadian voters would find it in their interest to wind up the plan would be delayed until 2030.

One effect of this kind of CPP reform is that the CPP fund would grow dramatically, much as, with UI benefits cut and premiums raised, the unemployment insurance fund has swelled. The CPP fund would quickly dwarf the $5–7 billion UI fund, however, rising to "$100 billion in 2007 and $200 billion in 2012" (p. 52). Robson predicts that, just as the buildup in the UI fund has prompted salivation among many interest groups, a political tug-of-war over what to do with the CPP fund will break out. He foresees the possibility, as allowed by the legislation that originally set up the CPP, of provinces' deciding to do as Quebec did from the outset and set up their own plans. This would be particularly attractive for provinces, such as Alberta, with favorable demographics and low debt ratios. As Robson puts it, "provincialization would be a logical response by certain provinces to paralysis or inadequate reform of the CPP" (p. 54).

A more extreme reform would be to do away with the Ponzi-like attributes of the pay-as-you-go CPP and move toward a fully funded system. The alternative of "coercing unwilling participants into the Ponzi scheme" with the reassurance that, under a new and improved scheme, they will lose only four and a half years' worth of earnings instead of six and a half is unlikely to be "a viable option" (p. 54). In preparation for privatization, Robson recommends "not only...improving the CPP's financial condition with fuller funding but...trimming it back and simultaneously improving the tax and regulatory treatment of private pension and registered retirement savings plans," thus gradually effecting a switchover from the CPP to these more private savings mechanisms (p. 55). He concludes with the following sobering thoughts:

> It is irresponsible of today's adults to try to impose the CPP on today's children and unrealistic to think that, when those children reach adulthood, they will accept the attempt if it is made. Canadians need to start preparing for a future without the CPP. (Ibid.)

Christopher Ragan:
Shut Down RRSPs, Raise the GST

As we have just seen, William Robson would like to expand RRSPs in anticipation of phasing out the Canada Pension Plan. Christopher Ragan, Associate Professor of Economics at McGill University, has quite a different plan for RRSPs. He wants to abolish them and replace them with consumption taxes. Like any good economist, Ragan is meticulous in setting out the logic of his argument: although tax-deferred savings plans (TDSPs), of which RRSP and RPPs are the best-known examples, very likely do not increase the overall amount of saving done by Canadians and their governments, they do cause a redistribution of wealth from lower-income to upper-income Canadians. They should therefore be replaced, Ragan says, by a package of complementary proposals that would encourage saving but would not send such a large gift to the upper regions of the income distribution.

As Ragan's introduction demonstrates, the RRSP stakes are considerable. In 1992, the annual flow of contributions into

RRSPs totaled $15 billion, compared with only $6.7 billion for RPPs, while the overall amount of wealth held in RRSPs is estimated at $220 billion in 1994. (The RRSP boom continued in 1995: total contributions were up 8 percent over the previous year, totaling $23 billion, although this was only 15 percent of the $153 billion in tax-deductible contributions Canadians could have made [Cohen 1996].) Of course, a main reason for the popularity of RRSPs is the favorable tax treatment they receive. Contributions can be deducted from taxable income, producing a current tax benefit equal to the taxpayer's marginal tax rate times whatever amount is contributed. Any investment income generated within the RRSP accumulates tax free until withdrawal, which can take place at any time, although for most people it occurs at retirement or shortly thereafter, with withdrawal obligatory by age 69.

Two hundred and twenty billion dollars is obviously a lot of money, and sounds as if it would have caused a substantial increase in Canada's capital stock, since much of the money Canadians put in their RRSPs is invested, either directly or through mutual funds, in the shares and bonds of companies whose business is accumulating real capital. Ragan argues, however, that TDSPs very likely *reduce* national saving. The reason is obvious once one realizes that national saving consists of saving by people and businesses but also by governments. In 1994, Canadian citizens and businesses between them saved 8.0 percent of GDP. Our deficit-ridden governments, on the other hand, "dissaved" 4.5 percent of GDP by spending more than they collected in taxes. What happens to national savings as a result of TDSPs depends on how they affect these three kinds of potential savers. People who invest in RRSPs almost certainly increase their overall saving as a result. Most people save at least something out of new income, and the tax breaks associated with TDSPs are like getting new income (even if, in reality, they merely let taxpayers keep old income). It is virtually certain that some of this new income is saved. On the other hand, it is also virtually certain that the provision of tax breaks reduces government saving (or, what is the same thing, increases government deficits). True, RRSPs drain away tax revenues both when contributions are made and when income accumulates tax free within the fund, but they boost tax revenues when withdrawals are made. Ragan calculates, however, that in 1992 the net loss to the federal government, even when taking the taxation of withdrawals into account, was $13 billion, with perhaps another $7 billion lost by the provinces. Ragan argues that this dissaving very likely offset any increase in saving out of the higher incomes of RRSP contributors.

That still might be good for national saving, however, if RRSPs had effectively turned Canada's income tax system into a consumption tax system. Economists generally favor the taxation of consumption rather than income for two reasons. First, much economic theory suggests that a society that discourages saving by taxing the interest, dividends, and capital gains it produces is like a farmer who eats his seed corn. Second, it is simply unfair that, of two people with the same assets today, the one who saves and earns a future income from them should be taxed more than the one who consumes them. Like most economists, Ragan accepts these arguments but argues that, if RRSPs are not completely comprehensive, so that any amount can be contributed to them, they are unlikely to produce the desired encouragement to saving. If they are to produce greater saving, they must induce a "substitution effect" — that is, they must raise the return to saving by reducing the taxes imposed on it. But a majority of Canadians do not have RRSPs, so the returns on whatever these people save are fully taxed. In the same way, Canadians who have hit their combined RRSP/RPP contribution limits also are fully taxed on any additional saving they do, for by definition that additional saving must occur outside their TDSPs. The only people who do not face full taxation of their savings at the margin are Canadians who have not hit their contribution limits and yet do all of their saving within their RRSPs and there simply may not be many such Canadians.

A third argument in favor of TDSPs such as the RRSP and RPP is that they encourage Canadians to save for their own retirement, thus reducing the need for government income support programs. On the other hand, they only *encourage* saving, they do not *require* it. Ragan argues that, if there is a real worry some Canadians will not bother to save because they know government stands ready to help them in their old age, the appropriate remedy is to force people to contribute to a reformed public pension system.

Although TDSPs have few social benefits, Ragan argues, they do have costs. *Somebody* pays for TDSPs. The tax revenue that is foregone has to be made up with other taxes, with reduced spending, higher borrowing, or the printing of money, which causes inflation. While it is theoretically possible that the only people who suffer from these changes are TDSP contributors, that would be something of a fluke. It is much more likely that nonbeneficiaries also pay, which means that the income redistribution that occurs is very probably perverse. Contributors to RRSPs generally have higher incomes than noncontributors. In 1991, for instance, only 24 percent of contributors had incomes less than $20,000 a year, while 12 percent had incomes higher than $60,000. Moreover, since they are in higher tax brackets, high-income contributors gain more from their contributions than low-income contributors. They also tend to contribute more than low-income contributors. As a result of both effects, contributors in 1991 who made more than $30,000 a year received a tax reduction averaging $879, while those making less than $30,000 a year received only $307. Ragan shows that, accumulated over many years, these differing benefits can add up to tens of thousands of dollars. "[I]t is unlikely," Ragan concludes, "that the typical Canadian would view TDSPs as a valuable instrument for improving the distribution of income" (p. 79).

What would Ragan do? First, he would end tax support for all tax-deferred savings plans, "including RRSPs, firm-sponsored pension plans, and the superannuation plans for the public service" (p. 81). Contributions to TDSPs no longer would be tax deductible, while their earnings would immediately be subject to tax. Employer contributions to defined-contribution pension plans no longer would be tax deductible, while employee contributions would not be excluded from taxable income. Anticipated benefits from defined-benefit plans could be "converted into an equivalent to current income that is taxable along with other current income" (ibid.). In effect, employer and employee contributions to pension plans would be treated as "ordinary payments to workers."

Second, Ragan would move toward a consumption-tax system by reducing income tax rates across the board and simultaneously increasing the goods and services tax (GST) rate (p. 83). At the same time, he would eliminate exemptions from the GST, such as groceries, thus dramatically reducing the system's administrative costs. Any undesirable redistributive effects that might result presumably could be avoided by increasing the generosity of the GST tax credit, which goes only to low-income Canadians. Ragan would not eliminate the income system entirely, however, as in his view it constitutes a useful administrative device for identifying those who need public income assistance.

Finally, Ragan would increase the role of mandatory saving, so as to reduce the need for the government to bail out low-income seniors. He would move toward a public saving system that was more fully funded; moreover, "there is no reason the management of these funds could not be entirely beyond the reach of government. They could be invested in private mutual funds and managed professionally" (p. 86).

Ragan closes his paper with what he calls a "crucial caveat" — that none of his recommendations be regarded as motivated by the need to reduce government deficits: since the abolition of TDSPs

> would represent a significant increase in the overall taxation of households....[t]he combination of...abolishing TDSPs plus lowering income tax rates and raising the GST...should be approximately revenue neutral. (Pp. 87–88.)

John Burbidge:
Reality Checks for Retirement Policies

John Burbidge, Professor of Economics at McMaster University, helps the debate along by looking at the economic underpinnings of the Canadian retirement system. Though he does not recommend specific reforms, he argues that the public pension system, which includes Old Age Security (OAS), the Guaranteed Income Supplement (GIS), and the age exemption (soon to be combined into Ottawa's proposed Seniors Benefit), together with the CPP and tax assistance for RPPs and RRSPs, should be made more "feasible." In other words, the system should better reflect taxpayers' ability to finance it.

One way to do this would be to link the growth of various pension payments, not to the consumer price index (CPI) nor even to the overall rate of economic growth, but to the growth of average or median wages. As Burbidge puts it, "stagnant or falling real earnings of prime-age workers since the mid-1970s imply that the set of intergenerational transfers feasible in the long term today is smaller than it was 20 years ago" (p. 94). Comparing the varying fortunes of pension recipients and prime-age workers over the last two decades, Burbidge finds that, measured in 1993 dollars, OAS payments rose by roughly $300 a month through the 1970s and since 1980 have been roughly constant in real terms. GIS payments rose sharply to the mid-1980s and since then have also been more or less constant. The Spousal Pension Allowance, introduced in 1975, provides additional benefits to younger spouses of retirees. Over roughly the same period, CPP benefits also became more generous as the plan was fully phased in and began to mature. In addition, in 1987 the CPP disability allowance was increased by $150 a month. As a result of these changes, the current retirement system "provides better insurance across and within generations" than did earlier systems, which before the 1960s were mainly private (p. 107). On the other hand, Canadians have been reluctant to back up their unquestioned generosity to seniors with the tax payments it requires, thus leaving the country with a debt problem. In addition, the difficulty of amending the CPP, which requires provincial approval in a formula much like the 1982 constitutional amending formula, means many of the more important changes to the retirement income system have been made via the purely federal OAS/GIS program. As a consequence, "Canada's system, dominated as it is by age-conditioned transfers..., differs markedly from the primarily earnings-related systems of most other countries, including the United States" (pp. 107–108). The GIS was supposed to be a temporary supplement until the CPP had matured but it is now a key part of the system. (Although the new Seniors Benefit ends its separate existence, the income-tested GIS lives on in the benefit's taxback provisions.)

After summarizing the economic literature on the important questions of whether old age security systems discourage either saving or labor supply, Burbidge finds reason for skepticism in both cases. The dramatic reduction in labor force participation rates among older men — from 50.4 percent in 1961 to 16.6 percent in 1993 for men aged 65–69 and from 85.9 percent to 60.9 percent for those aged 55–64 — *is* consistent with the ideas both that public pension plans make older workers wealthier and that they discourage work by in effect taxing wages and salaries. In some cases, in fact, the combined taxback rate of public plans is greater than 100 percent, high enough to discourage anyone from working. On the other hand, Burbidge argues that, with the flood of baby boomers into the work force, many *private* pension plans were changed to encourage early retirement. Moreover, phasing in the CPP, which involved year-by-year increases in the proportion of pensionable earnings that would be paid out in pensions, created a strong incentive to delay retirement: "with the generosity of pensions increasing so quickly, working even a short while longer caused a sharp increase in retirement income" (pp. 112–113). Burbidge thinks it possible that work-discouraging changes in private pension plans could in fact be reversed over the next few decades as firms find themselves strapped for new workers: "Thus, some of the concern about the future high projected costs of caring for the elderly may be misplaced" (p. 113).

On the problem of savings, Burbidge contrasts the views of Harvard University's Robert Barro with those of Feldstein, whose work has already been mentioned. In a famous article published in 1974, Feldstein argued that social security payments had caused a large reduction in overall US saving, since workers felt the government would take care of a major part of their retirement needs. Barro, on the other hand, argued that public retirement pensions could have almost no effect on overall saving since the final decision as to how much older citizens consume lies with their families. If governments encourage more consumption by seniors than families think warranted, they can reduce their assistance to their senior members. Thus, if the government encourages "dissaving" — that is, greater consumption by seniors — families can offset this by doing more saving of their own. In the limit, Burbidge explains, "the private offset matches the public transfer dollar for dollar, leaving the consumption level of both young and old unchanged" (p. 114). Burbidge's own work indicates Canadian seniors do more saving than had been thought. In fact, saving *increases* slightly with age, which suggests that when resources are transferred to seniors the overall saving rate may not suffer.

Burbidge closes, not with specific policy proposals, but with candidates for further study. He notes that pre-tax annual incomes of urban married-couple families in which the husband was retired were 50 percent higher in real terms in 1989 than they had been in 1976, while over the same period real earnings for full-time, full-year workers either stagnated or declined over the period. He thus argues that "[g]overnment-mandated intergenerational transfers to the elderly should be brought into line with what working-age generations can afford and wish to provide" (p. 124). Where should cuts come from? Not from the OAS/GIS system, since the GIS is already income tested, while the Mulroney government began the clawback of OAS payments. (The new income-tested

Seniors Benefit confirms Burbidge's prediction that assistance targeted mainly at lower-income elders should not be reduced.) That leaves either RRSPs or the CPP. Since RRSPs are linked to pension rules so as to provide fairness between those who do and do not have private pensions, Burbidge argues that major changes will come through the CPP.

One possibility is to phase out the CPP over ten years. The blow for lower-income seniors would be cushioned by income-tested demogrants, while the higher-income seniors who clearly would suffer would at least be spared radical RRSP reform. Younger Canadians, as Robson's numbers suggest, would likely benefit from such a change.

A second possibility is to condition the overall amount spent on demogrants for elders — the new Seniors Benefit, basically — on the growth of the real earnings of the workers who must finance it. This would prevent discretionary increases in the well-being of seniors, and if it meant they could not do substantially better than the people who were financing their pensions, they also could not do substantially worse. In closing, however, Burbidge warns that "much more work is required to understand what the effects of this structural change would be" (p. 126).

Lam, Prince, and Cutt: Simulating the Future, Restoring the CPP

Newman Lam, Michael J. Prince, and James Cutt, who all teach public policy and administration at the University of Victoria, take a look at the program details and financing dynamics of the CPP, which they see as a "part of Canada's heritage that is worth keeping but needs prompt renovation" (p. 129). Fortunately, "fairly simple corrective measures do exist" (ibid.).

At the moment, Canadian workers and their employers each pay 2.8 percent of the employees' earnings into the CPP, up to the "year's maximum pensionable earnings," which is roughly related to the average industrial wage. The first 10 percent of earnings are exempt, however. Make at least ten years of contributions and you are entitled to a pension. What you get is one-quarter of the average "year's maximum pensionable earnings" in the three years before you retire, times your "earnings ratio." Your earnings ratio is whatever you earned in a month, divided by maximum pensionable earnings for that month, averaged over your entire working life. In calculating the average, however, you get to drop any time during which you were either over 65 or had at least one child less than seven years of age. You can also choose to drop another 15 percent of your earnings months, provided this still leaves you with ten years of contributions. The purpose of dropping months, of course, is to raise your earnings ratio: in fact, you only drop them if doing so achieves this. The earnings ratio thus provides a connection between what you paid into the plan and what you get out of it. But the connection is a loose one: if you are lucky enough to retire when maximum pensionable earnings are rising rapidly, you get more out of the plan than you paid in.

Lam, Prince, and Cutt note that the folklore of the CPP is that the plan is in trouble because of the baby boom, which will soon cause a sharp increase in the proportion of Canada's population aged 65 and over. On the other hand, CPP payouts began to exceed contributions as early as 1984, when the first of the baby boomers were just turning 40 and entering their prime earning years. The obvious conclusion is that, although population aging "does have serious implications for the CPP[,]...that challenge is not the only reason for the plan's financial problems. They are, in fact, caused by a number of factors that have reduced revenues and increased expenditures" (pp. 135–136). Among these other contributing factors, Lam, Prince, and Cutt identify a "low contribution rate, low returns on CPP investments, increased CPP benefits, rapid increases in the upper limit on pensionable earnings..., and the short contributory period for entitlement to a full pension" (p. 136). They proceed to run computer simulations examining the influence of each of these factors.

The first factor is the plan's low contribution rate, which started in 1966 at 3.6 percent and remained there for 21 years, even though, "[i]n 1975, survivor benefits were provided to widowers as well as widows, retirement and earnings tests were dropped for retirement benefits, and all CPP benefits were fully indexed to increases in the CPI" (p. 139) and, in 1978, the option of dropping low-income months from the formula was introduced.

The CPP also suffers from low real rates of return — an average of 1.5 percent — on its investment funds. By 1989, a dollar that in 1967 had been placed in provincial bonds, the CPP's only permitted investments, was worth $5.41. Placed in private investment funds, it would have been worth $8.60. Finally, the granting of full pension rights on the basis of only ten years of contributions meant the plan was bound to experience difficulty. In fact, Lam, Prince, and Cutt show that "even a full 30 years of contributions is insufficient to finance today's retirement pensions (much less other benefits, such as survivor and disability benefits)" (pp. 144–145).

What can be done? One obvious option is to raise the contribution rate. Assuming a 2 percent real rate of return on investments, a life expectancy of 85 years, and a contributory period of fully 40 years, the authors calculate that a contribution rate of 7 percent (1.4 percentage points higher than today's 5.6 percent) would be required to fully finance the current average retirement pension of $8,600 per year. Survivors and disability benefits would take that to 10 or 11 percent, however, although Lam, Prince, and Cutt recommend that these in fact be paid for by workers' compensation or out of general revenues. Eliminating exemption of the first 10 percent of a worker's earnings would increase the accumulated funds available for the payment of his or her pension by more than 12 percent at the age of 65. On the other hand, as British Columbia has pointed out in recent federal-provincial discussions on pensions, the attendant rise in taxes would impose a proportionately greater burden on low-income workers.

Lam, Prince, and Cutt also find big payoffs to making a wider array of investments available to the CPP's managers: "for every percentage point increase in real return, the accumulated funds [at retirement] increase by 20 percent or more" (p. 152). They also suggest serious consideration be given to reforms that would give plan holders — that is, the general public — more control over investment decisions, and possibly even hand over control of the fund to an independent authority.

Another obvious way to improve the financial health of the CPP would be to reduce benefits. Though Lam, Prince, and Cutt note that, in 1992, retirees were only 8.0 percent of poor Canadians, compared with 20.4 percent just ten years earlier, they judge that directly reducing benefits would be "politically difficult" (p. 154). One way to reduce them indirectly, however, would be to raise the minimum contribution period that entitles contributors to a full benefit, a change that would not necessarily be unfair, since "individuals with a shorter contributory period are not necessarily the most in need" (ibid.). The authors note that to finance the current average annual pension of $8,600 with only ten years of contributions requires a real rate of return on investment of 14.4 percent, which is much higher than the long-term Canadian average. With a contribution period of 40 years, by contrast, a return of only 2.1 percent provides full financing. To put it another way, a five-year reduction of the contributory period from 40 years to 35 years reduces the pension funds available at age 65 by 10.6 percent.

Yet another way to improve the CPP's financial health would be to eliminate the dropout provision that allows people to delete their worst earning years when calculating their earning ratio. Lam, Prince, and Cutt calculate that this would reduce the value of CPP entitlements at age 65 by 3 to 6 percent. An option that would improve the CPP's finances more significantly would be to raise the retirement age to, say, 70, which would simultaneously shorten the payout period and lengthen the contribution period by five years. It would also provide five more years in which investment returns could compound themselves. The overall result, the authors figure, would be an 80 percent increase in the accumulated pension funds available at retirement. The downside, of course, is that it would require five more years of work from senior citizens.

On balance, Lam, Prince, and Cutt argue that clawing back CPP benefits would be unfair since, rightly or wrongly, people regard them as having been earned by contributions. On the other hand, it might be possible politically to sell the idea of de-indexing CPP payouts and instead having an independent committee decide how much of an increase was justified at any time, given the overall economic climate. The authors also suggest the possibility of tying benefits, not to the average industrial wage, but to the rate of inflation, which is forecast to grow more slowly than wages over the next few years. They calculate that, if contributions grow with wages but benefits grow with prices, the saving would be fully 65 percent of funds accumulated at age 65.

After considering these many possibilities, Lam, Prince, and Cutt favor a five-part package:

- Quickly raise the combined employer/employee contribution rate to 8 percent, which would be sufficient to raise more than 14 percent in additional funds over the contribution period and, with the other measures they recommend, pay off the existing unfunded liability.

- Invest contributions through the capital market under the supervision of an independent authority "set up to regulate investment activities and to protect the interest of contributors" (p. 164).

- Gradually raise the retirement age for full pension entitlement to 70 years. Phasing this in over 25 years could bring an overall improvement of almost 80 percent in the funds available at retirement.

- Freeze the retirement pension at its current level of purchasing power, which could increase funds available by fully two-thirds.

- Remove survivor and disability benefits from the CPP and provide them through workers' compensation or the Seniors

Benefit. In fact, unless these programs are moved out of the CPP — which, after all, is supposed to be a contributory pension, not a social insurance program — the first four recommended measures would not in fact bring the plan into balance.

In their overall effect, Lam, Prince, and Cutt conclude: "[t]he recommended policy options should be able to provide enough funds to finance the CPP pensions with a surplus to absorb the existing unfunded liabilities" (p. 166). They end by suggesting that the national project of restoring the CPP to health in the 1990s "could help revive Canadians' collective sense of themselves in the pursuit of peace, order, and good government as well as dignity and security in old age" (p. 168).

Paul Dickinson:
Six Common Misperceptions about the CPP

Paul Dickinson teaches economics at McGill University and has written extensively on questions of Canadian social policy. Here, he attempts to set the record straight on the status quo, or at least the status quo as it existed before the federal government announced the new Seniors Benefit. Dickinson neither proposes nor defends any particular policies but instead tries to dispel six common misperceptions about Canada's retirement income system. In an area of study too often characterized by heated pronouncements about the imminent bankruptcy or collapse of this or that program, but especially of the "unfunded" CPP, Dickinson's phlegmatic approach is like a welcome breeze on a hot summer day. It is also in many ways persuasive.

The first misperception Dickinson addresses is that the retirement system brings about a perverse redistribution of income by giving generous handouts to retired Canadians who are, by and large, no worse off than the rest of the population. He argues, first, that the criticism is irrelevant to the CPP and QPP, which are designed to replace wage earners' incomes, not to guarantee a minimal level of retirement income for poor seniors, which is the job of OAS/GIS. "To complain that the CPP pays pensions to high-income retirees is like complaining that private pension plans pay bigger pensions to people who contribute more to them" (p. 185). If people contributed to the CPP, they have a right to benefits. More fundamentally, Dickinson argues that the attack's premise is wrong: while the vast majority of seniors are now above Statistics Canada's "low-income cutoff" (what people normally refer to as "the poverty line"), many are only just above it, and this only because of old age assistance. In 1994, only one in eight households containing a senior had family income greater than $50,000. Finally, Dickinson notes that the degree of redistribution effected by the CPP is much greater than the simple spending numbers suggest: simulations on 1993 data indicate that 40 percent of benefits is effectively returned to governments in the form of taxes or reductions in other programs, especially OAS/GIS.

A second misperception is that contribution rates to the CPP are seriously regressive and will become more so as these rates rise over the next decade to finance perceived shortfalls in CPP funding. Dickinson takes on several aspects of this misperception. To begin with, although the current CPP contribution rate is 5.6 percent of earnings (and is expected to increase to almost 14 percent by 2030), no one actually pays (or would pay) this rate. The first 10 percent of earnings is exempted, so at most people pay 90 percent of 5.6 (or 14) percent. Moreover, both Ottawa and the provinces provide a tax credit for CPP contributions, thus giving a partial rebate of income taxes. Finally, contributions are not levied on all earnings, but rather on earnings up to a maximum. Anyone who earns precisely the maximum will pay taxes equal to the statutory values (subject to the preceding qualifications), but people who earn more than that pay no tax on their extra earnings, which has the effect of reducing their overall liability. Dickinson notes that, at 180 percent of the Year's Maximum Pensionable Earnings ($61,920 in 1994), employee contributions paid at the 13.04 percent rate projected for 2030 would in fact equal only 2.39 percent of earnings after income taxes. This rate could be even lower if it went to finance only the retirement income proportion of CPP payouts, but in fact something less than two-thirds of CPP payouts is for traditional retirement benefits, while the other one-third goes to disability, survivor, death, and orphan benefits, as well as administrative costs. At bottom, however, Dickinson rejects the progressivity/regressivity argument, since it applies to taxes, while contributions that give rise to tied benefits are not taxes.

A third perceived fault of the CPP is that low-income seniors do not receive benefits, no matter how much they have contributed. The reason is that other parts of the retirement income system, most notably the GIS and, in Ontario, GAINS-A, are reduced by whatever other income seniors may receive, including CPP benefits. Here, Dickinson argues that the system must be seen in its entirety. As a whole, it certainly does get money to low-income seniors; in fact, it is the main reason most seniors are above the poverty line. It is also true that, if the GIS and GAINS-A are regarded as the frontline of the system, then their effective taxation of other income does mean that no such income, including CPP payments, gets to low-income seniors. But Dickinson argues that this is an "upside-down" view of the system. If the CPP is regarded as the system's frontline — which, as a contributory pension scheme designed to replace earnings, it should be — then, in effect, low-income Canadians' prior receipt of CPP payments causes their incomes to rise to the point where they are prevented from getting these other forms of support, rather than these other forms of support preventing them from getting CPP payments.

A fourth misperception about the CPP is that future generations of contributors will be either unwilling or unable to finance future payouts. Where today there are five people of working age for every senior, in 2030 there are expected to be only three. On the other hand, if productivity grows at the 1 percent annual rate that the official projections forecast, future workers will be richer than today's workers and therefore better able to support a larger retired population at a given absolute standard of living. Moreover, Dickinson argues, while Canada's *retired* population will be larger than it is today, its *dependent* population may not be. In effect, financially dependent children and teenagers will be replaced by financially dependent seniors. It is true that more of the burden of financing young people has been borne privately, rather than publicly, but if private burdens fall, there may be more room for the assumption of public ones. It is also possible that the work force will continue to grow in relation to the overall population. In fact, if the labor force participation rate of Canadian women were to reach the current male rate, in 2021 the overall dependency ratio would be the same as it is now. Dickinson concludes this section of the argument by looking at what happens to the real disposable incomes of future taxpayers under certain assumptions about future taxes and economic growth. If real economic growth proceeds at 1 percent a year and if tax brackets are adjusted to keep overall revenues constant at 22 percent of earnings at the maximum CPP earnings level, then the real disposable earnings of such workers increase by more than a third between 1992 and 2030, while tax revenues rise by 40 percent. It appears there is ample room to finance both a reasonable return on the CPP and at least respectable growth in real, after-tax incomes.

The fifth and perhaps most widely held misperception about the CPP is that it offers current contributors a very low, perhaps even negative, real rate of return on their savings. As Dickinson notes, it has been widely reported that people born in 1980 will receive one dollar of CPP benefits for each dollar they contribute and that people born in 2000 will receive only 80 cents (p. 204), a raw deal by almost anyone's standards, especially when the CPP's original recipients have done very well out of the program. In Dickinson's view, there are several dimensions to this misperception. First, the fact that, beginning in 1976, Canadians who had contributed to CPP for only ten years were able to retire with full benefits meant that these original contributors did very well, earning real returns on their savings of almost 20 percent. But they are not a continuing burden on the plan: by 2005 they will be roughly 95 years old, and the pensions of 95-year-olds account for less than one-twentieth of a percentage point of future contribution rates. By contrast, people who retire at age 65 in 2005 will have been paying in for almost 40 years and will receive a much lower real rate of return. Young workers of that day will not be financing "gold-plated" pensions for their elders. So what kind of plating *will* future pensions have? Many Canadians apparently anticipate lead-plating, but Dickinson argues that this is partly because they confuse the insurance and pension features of the CPP. When the disability insurance component of contributions is excluded, the retirement return on the employee's share of contributions for members of the cohort born in 1974 (today's 22-year-olds) exceeds 7 percent (7.68 percent) if they live to age 80, and is almost 8 percent (7.92 percent) if they live to age 85. Since these calculations assume an average future inflation rate of 3.5 percent, the corresponding real rates of return are 3.73 percent and 4.42 percent, respectively. These rates, however, are for people who earn the CPP maximum earnings. People who earn only half of maximum earnings would experience real rates of return that are higher still (4.18 percent at age 80, 4.83 percent at age 85). Of course, the real returns are lower for self-employed workers, who pay both the employer's and employee's shares of contributions — approximately 1 percent (0.97 percent) at age 80, and 2 percent (1.9 percent) at age 85. These may or may not be competitive with what could be earned by private pension plans, but the nominal returns are certainly not zero or less.

The last misperception Dickinson addresses is the doomsday question: Is the CPP fiscally viable? In other words, will the plan go broke? Dickinson answers that it is very misleading to use "bankruptcy" in the context of the CPP, since it is basically a pay-as-you-go plan. CPP benefits are paid mainly out of current contributions, so if contributors decide they no longer wish to contribute, or wish to contribute less, then beneficiaries will have to make do with less than they had expected to receive. But precisely because the CPP is not fully funded, it cannot "go broke." True, at the end of 1992 assets in the CPP Account covered only about 8.5 percent of total future obligations, but "[t]he account is a small proportion of the total liability because the plan was designed that way, not because it is going broke" (p. 214). Dickinson argues that the CPP's "unfundedness" should be seen in perspective. OAS payments (since folded into the Seniors Benefit) are widely expected to be there when future seniors become eligible for them and they therefore constitute an informal unfunded liability of the federal government, but "government accounting methods do not ask how much money is needed now to finance such programs for the next 50 years" (p. 215). Contrasting the CPP with the national debt, which clearly is a legal obligation to pay, Dickinson notes that, while the debt has already been spent, the CPP's unfunded liability has yet to be spent. In Dickinson's view, changes to the CPP formula that would cause less money to be spent would not necessarily violate the spirit of public pension programs. In a comment very much in accord with Burbidge's message, Dickinson closes by noting that public pensions are contingent promises linking the standard of living of pensioners to the general standard of living, and their contingent formulas may have to change in response to other economic and fiscal pressures.

In sum, while Dickinson is not opposed to changes in the current retirement income system — and in fact suggests change will be a normal state of affairs for any such system — he believes changes should be founded in a sound perception of reality, not in misperception. That is an instructive coda both for his paper and for this book.

William Watson

References

Cohen, Bruce. 1996. "RRSP contributions up again." *Financial Post*, October 22.

Feldstein, Martin. 1996. "Social Security and Saving: New Time Series Evidence." *National Tax Journal* 49 (2): 151–164.

Ponzi's Pawns:
Young Canadians and the Canada Pension Plan

William B.P. Robson

In December 1919, Charles Ponzi, a small-time swindler recently out of jail and working in Boston as a clerk for a firm of import-export brokers, made an intriguing discovery while conducting company business at the post office. The rate at which postal-reply coupons bought in Europe were redeemable for stamps at US post offices had been fixed by treaty before World War I, but subsequent changes in exchange rates had raised their purchasing power in the United States to multiples of their cost in Europe. A few trial runs in which a partner bought coupons in Spain and Ponzi redeemed them at home produced almost ten-for-one profits.

So Ponzi left the import-export firm for a new career. Establishing an office in fortuitously named Pie Alley, he advertised with the slogan, "50 percent profit on your money in 45 days; double it in 6 months." Money from investors began to pour in. As Ponzi's fortune and fame rocketed upward, he soon found that the volume of money coming in exceeded what could be cycled through the postal coupon scheme. Undaunted, he began simply passing the funds of new investors along as dividends to earlier ones.

Without implying any responsibility for flaws or peculiar opinions in this paper, I thank Ken Boessenkool, Bernard Dussault, Michael Grant, Angela Ferrante, Malcolm Hamilton, David Laidler, Phil Oreopoulos, John Robson, Bill Scarth, Peter Townley, and the series editors, John Richards and Bill Watson, for helpful comments and insightful queries.

After a few months, the massive discrepancy between the money invested in Ponzi's company and the actual issue of postal-reply coupons began to arouse suspicions. Ponzi's skill as a con man and the considerable following he had gained among early investors allowed him to brazen his way through until August 1920. By then, however, Montreal police (whose previous dealings with Ponzi had culminated in his receiving a three-year prison term for forgery) had alerted US officials as to his identity. His assets were impounded, and he was arrested — though not without physical attacks on the police by the enthusiastic investors waiting in his office at the time.

Some participants in Ponzi's scheme continued to regard him as a financial genius, but his reputation was damaged by large losses and the subsequent legal proceedings. When he was released after more than a decade in prison, he had to be given a police escort to protect him from a hostile mob. He then lapsed into relative obscurity and died in 1949 at age 66, leaving two legacies: enough money for a pauper's funeral, and a new name for one of the world's oldest financial scams: the "Ponzi game."[1]

The Ponzi Game

The essence of a Ponzi game is that each participant's returns are paid not from investment proceeds but from a later participant's investment. Chain letters and pyramid schemes are classic examples.

For a scam of this type to work, the new funds flowing in must always be sufficient to allow returns to previous investors that exceed what would be available from investments in bonds, shares, real estate, and so on. If the flow of funds shrinks to the point at which normal investments become more attractive, no new participants can be enticed in, the flow of fresh funds dries up, and the scheme collapses. A Ponzi game thus requires either

---

[1] For more details on Ponzi's career, see Deeson (1971, 115–125).

that investors who contribute a specified amount grow in number over time at a rate higher than the rate of return on alternative investments or, to the extent that the increase in investors falls short of the alternative rate of return, that each set of investors put in more money than its predecessors.

Canada's Biggest Ponzi Game

The boom-and-bust life cycle of Ponzi schemes is a reminder that the circumstances to support one are unusual. The lure of quick riches is intense, however, and in the mid-1960s, governments in Canada and most other developed countries thought that the right circumstances had arrived for a particularly ambitious version of a Ponzi scheme. Thanks to the baby boom, the labor force was growing rapidly. For reasons still debated by economic historians, growth in productivity and hence incomes was very robust. At the same time, returns to saving were relatively low — some three percentage points below economic growth rates.

In that environment, it looked possible to create social security systems that would pay retirement pensions and other benefits not from nest eggs built up in funded plans but from the taxes of younger workers. So Canada, like other developed democracies, took the pay-as-you-go Ponzi approach to the new income replacement tier of its public pension system, putting the Canada Pension Plan (CPP) in place alongside the pay-as-you-go income support tier of the Old Age Security program, the Guaranteed Income Supplement, and the Spouses' Allowance.[2]

Projecting the circumstances of the time forward, the CPP's designers thought they had a system with all of a Ponzi game's attractions but without its fatal flaws. The first cohorts of participants could be given payouts enormously in excess of what investment in a normal funded plan could provide — an especially

---

2 The income support programs do not pay benefits linked (even tenuously) to contributions. As discussed further below, parallel Ponzi-style criticisms are not apt in their case.

attractive feature at a time when the then-elderly had had a large part of their prime working years disrupted by depression and war.[3] Their immediate successors, with somewhat longer contribution periods, could receive less spectacular but still attractive payouts. And once the plan was mature, in the sense that all benefit recipients had contributed for their entire working lifetimes, returns would still be marginally superior to those available in a funded plan, since a growing population and rapidly rising incomes per person would provide fresh funds in amounts greater than could be provided by regular investments.

A state-run Ponzi game had the further advantage of coercive power. Since participation could be made mandatory, the critical issue of confidence among current and future players appeared less pressing. As Nobel Prize–winning economist Paul Samuelson put it, "[a] growing nation is the greatest Ponzi game ever contrived" (1967, 88).

Reluctant Players

Experience since the CPP's inception has highlighted the unusual nature of the circumstances in which it was created. Population and productivity growth rates have both dropped back to levels more typical of longer-term historical experience. At the same time, returns to saving have risen. The anomalous margin of economic growth over returns to saving that prevailed during the quarter-century following World War II has disappeared, giving way to a more normal premium of investment returns over growth rates.

Perhaps confident in their ability to continue coercing future participants into the plan over the long term, the CPP's masters

---

3 Citing this fact in defense of the CPP's *current* operations is suspect, however. Those reaching the age of eligibility for full CPP retirement benefits in 1996 — who, as shown below, will do very well out of the plan at their childrens' and grandchildrens' expense — were still in elementary school when the depression ended, and most did not begin full-time work until well after World War II was over.

have reacted to the disappearance of the circumstances needed for a Ponzi game's survival with incremental moves to enhance the benefits of participation to those already in. Benefits have been enriched and eligibility for them expanded. The resulting rise in the plan's long-term costs, especially in connection with disability benefits, has been startling. When the CPP was established, the benefits projected for 2030 were expected to cost an amount equal to some 5.5 percent of contributory earnings (the aggregate base on which contributions are calculated) — that is, aggregate earnings between the Year's Basic Exemption (YBE) and the Year's Maximum Pensionable Earnings (YMPE). The latest projections are for benefit costs equal to 14.2 percent of contributory earnings, with benefit enrichment accounting for nearly half the increase.[4] And contribution rates have been held down. If the 25-year contribution rate schedule set by the federal and provincial finance ministers in 1991 is adhered to, the two-year buffer of funds held in the CPP account will be exhausted in 20 years' time, and the resulting need to replenish it in subsequent years will boost the contribution rate in 2030 to almost 15.5 percent (Canada 1995, 6–7). (Box 1 provides definitions and more discussion of various contribution rates.)

Inherent in this situation are temptations for politicians and bureaucrats to make soothing but misleading statements. When returns to saving exceed economic growth rates, a Ponzi-style pension plan *cannot* make everyone better off indefinitely. For a time, the promises to soon-to-be-beneficiaries can be enriched in order to keep their returns from participation superior to what they could get by saving outside the plan. Doing so, however, entails a commitment to take more away from younger workers, children, and the unborn, whose benefits are still a long way off.

---

4 If higher projected disability costs as a result of benefit liberalization are added to other benefit enrichments, their combined contribution to the increase in the cost of benefits as a proportion of contributory earnings in 2030 is 3.9 percentage points (Governments of Canada 1996, 4).

**Box 1: *Pay-As-You-Go, Current, and
            Default Contribution Schedules***

The ratio of benefit costs to contributory earnings is often called the
pay-as-you-go rate, since it is equal to the contribution rate that would
need to be charged if each year's inflow of contributions exactly equaled
each year's payout of benefits, and the funds in the CPP account were
always equal to zero (so that none of the cost of benefits was covered by
investment earnings). Governments of Canada (1996, 20) provides a
summary of the changes in pay-as-you-go rates resulting from various
changes, based on reports from the chief actuary.

In fact, the CPP account is generally intended to contain the equivalent of two years' payouts. As noted in the text, the *current contribution
schedule* is now projected to be insufficient to keep the CPP account
positive. It is now under review.

Absent agreed changes, the CPP legislation provides for *default
contribution rates* according to a formula that, at five-year intervals, sets
future contribution rates such that, at the end of a 15-year period, the
CPP account will contain at least two years' payout. The chief actuary's
most recent report calculates that this formula would produce CPP
contributions that, over the 1997–2015 period, would average a little
more than one percentage point higher than under the current schedule.
Under this scenario, the account would remain positive, and the contribution rate in 2030 would be 13.9 percent (Canada 1995, 2–3, 29).

The pay-as-you-go, current, and default schedules of contribution
rates are illustrated in the figure below.

CPP Contribution Rates, 1970–2070

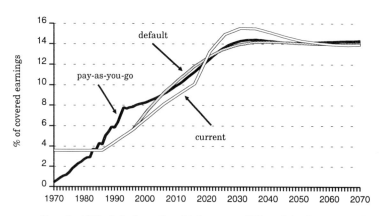

Sources: Canada 1995; data from the chief actuary, Office of the Superintendent of
          Financial Institutions, Canada.

Such a strategy ultimately must fail since contributions cannot rise indefinitely. Moreover, as with any Ponzi scheme, expectations of collapse over the longer term will hasten that collapse, as participants increasingly doubtful of receiving benefits begin to resist paying in. Hence, the CPP's administrators make strong statements about their commitment to the plan and its permanence as part of the Canadian policy scene. For example, a recent federal-provincial-territorial discussion paper on the CPP's problems starts a chapter entitled "CPP: The Issues Facing Us Today" by saying, "[t]he CPP is today and will continue to be a key pillar of Canada's retirement income system" (Governments of Canada 1996, 19).

Though understandable as products of political necessity, such statements are a weak foundation for a young Canadian's retirement planning.

Dangers and Opportunities

In the next section of this paper, I argue that the CPP will be hard pressed to survive the baby boomers' retirement in anything like its current form. Today's children might be willing to forgo a portion of the higher returns available from saving outside the CPP for the sake of its broad insurance features and other redistributive aspects. The size of the benefits that older Canadians have promised themselves, however, makes the penalty associated with participation in an unreformed CPP so large as to be measurable in *years* of covered earnings effectively confiscated. Older Canadians may attempt to force their children into such a system, but an analysis of likely voting patterns as the really big losers from the system reach adulthood suggests that an unreformed CPP will almost certainly not survive.

I then turn to some suggestions for reform. Drawing from proposals in the recent governmental discussion paper (ibid., 27–29), I consider a ten-year move to a much higher contribution rate, one that would keep the CPP account positive indefinitely, as well as a ten-year scaling back of benefits by 10 percent.[5] Both changes would reduce the penalty that the CPP is projected to impose on the young and improve its chances of surviving the baby boomers' retirement. The size of the improvement is disappointing, however, and it is bought with a sizable deterioration in the prospects for the baby boomers themselves — a situation that might, in turn, give rise to new demands for re-enrichment of benefits, returning us to a situation not unlike today's. It seems wise, therefore, to contemplate more radical reforms, perhaps on a province-by-province basis, that would do away with the CPP's current structure, pay accrued benefits from regular federal and/ or provincial budgets, and provide future benefits from a funded system involving more individual responsibility and control.

The Hazards of Being Late

That the CPP is a bad deal for younger Canadians is no longer news. Its unfairness was a core theme of a recent paper from the Canadian Youth Foundation (Grant 1996). Even the intergovernmental discussion paper on CPP reform (Government of Canada, 4) acknowledges at the outset that younger Canadians will be asked to pay many times more than their parents and grandparents did for a comparable package of benefits.

A dramatic illustration of the CPP's poor treatment of younger generations is provided by Ottawa's chief actuary, who has calculated nominal internal rates of return on CPP participation — the implicit return, expressed at annual rates, on all contributions to the plan — for each cohort based on the actual or projected experience of an average participant. (The full amount of CPP contributions, including the employer-paid portion, is treated by the chief actuary and in this paper as a tax on the worker. This

---

5 The federal-provincial-territorial discussion paper describes these changes for illustrative purposes, not as specific proposals, and it mentions no time frame for them. Private conversations with the Department of Finance, however, indicate that they were envisioned as being phased in over ten years.

assumption is common in evaluating the longer-term impact of payroll taxes, which is generally to depress wages dollar for dollar — an outcome that must seem unremarkable to the 10 percent of CPP contributors who are self-employed.) These figures show that the first cohort eligible for full retirement benefits, those who reached age 65 in 1976, received an implicit annual return of more than 30 percent on their contributions, far superior to what they could have earned by making the same contributions to a funded plan. By contrast, average participants born in 1988 are expected to receive a return about one-sixth as high — 5.2 percent, which is barely more than 1.5 percent after allowing for projected inflation[6] and much less than they could reasonably expect to earn in alternative investments (Canada 1995, 101).[7]

Low Returns for the Young

The clearest way to illustrate the CPP's different treatment of various age cohorts is to show how representative participants would fare depending on year of birth.

In working out my projections, I accepted the basic assumptions of the chief actuary (Canada 1995) for the projection period:

- annual inflation of 3.5 percent;
- nominal wage growth of 4.5 percent annually; and
- a nominal annual return on invested funds of 6.0 percent (roughly 2.5 percent in real terms).

---

6 Because CPP entitlements and benefits are indexed to inflation, changing the 3.5 percent inflation assumption used in the chief actuary's calculations (and in the simulations reported below) would not influence these projections as long as the real interest rate is held constant.

7 The full impact of CPP participation is now even worse for many of these individuals because contributions receive relief from personal income tax only at the lowest marginal rate — a bias that did not affect earlier participants — while their benefits will trigger clawbacks that amount to much higher marginal tax rates than was the case for early recipients.

And I used a life profile in which the representative participant:

- earns at or above the YMPE from age 23 to age 62;
- becomes disabled at age 62 and collects CPP disability benefits until age 65;[8]
- collects regular retirement benefits for a period calibrated to projected life expectancies at age 65, a period that varies with year of birth (later cohorts live longer); and
- dies, triggering a death benefit and five years' worth of survivor benefits for a spouse.

The resulting profile of contributions and benefits is consistent with the chief actuary's projections of the expected experience of a composite CPP participant about to enter the plan. Such an individual born in 1976 and entering the CPP in 1999 would need to pay a contribution rate marginally over 10.5 percent through his or her participation in the plan to exactly cover the cost of all the benefits to which that participation would give rise.

Figure 1 shows the implicit annualized nominal return on the CPP contributions of cohorts of such participants spaced five years apart, ranging from the earliest group to receive full benefits, in 1976, to its equivalent a century later. (The calculation is on the basis of the *default contribution schedule* that will prevail in the absence of agreement on CPP reforms — see Box 1.)

These implicit returns do not necessarily correspond to the experience of any single individual. They have the advantage, however, of showing how CPP participation affects those who differ only in their life expectancy at age 65 and the contribution rates they face as a result of the timing of their participation.[9]

---

8 Rather than being a literal description of a typical participant's experience, this period of disability is a convenient way of representing the financial impact of various preretirement provisions, such as the general and child-rearing dropout periods, as well as disability benefits themselves.

9 Because CPP benefits have been enriched over the years and especially because earlier cohorts made less use of disability provisions, using average characteristics of projected *future* participants in this exercise exaggerates...

Figure 1: *Implicit Annualized Nominal Returns from CPP Participation*

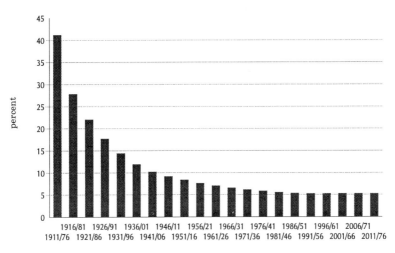

year of birth/retirement

Note: See text for assumptions and life profile of the average individual, who earns at or above the YMPE throughout his or her working life.

The comparatively meager returns to today's youngsters — barely 1.5 percent in real terms (recall the 3.5 percent inflation rate embodied in the projections) — are striking and ought to be more than a little embarrassing to earlier cohorts.

How Many Years' Earnings Will They Lose?

Figure 1 does not tell a complete story. Of greater interest is the size of the bonus or penalty that CPP participation provides

Note 9 - cont'd.

...the CPP's benefits to those in the more distant past. (Figure 1 shows 40 percent returns to the cohort that turned 65 in 1976, while the chief actuary calculated a figure of a little more than 30 percent; the discrepancy in later years is much smaller.) This bias does not affect the analysis of benefit gaps and voting patterns below, since the windup scenarios examined do not affect people already receiving retirement benefits.

relative to alternative income replacement plans. In this sense, the consequences of participation depend on two things: first, the returns participants might be able to earn by making their contributions to an alternative funded plan; second, the size of the contributions that they are expected to make — a poor return on a tiny investment being an altogether different matter from a poor return on a large one.

One way of getting a sense of the net impact of CPP participation on various cohorts is to calculate the retirement nest egg that a representative individual's premiums would buy at age 65 if they had accumulated in a funded plan.[10] The next step is to calculate the value of the benefit package promised by the CPP to that representative participant at age 65 — that is, what would a benefit package of equivalent value be worth as, say, a registered retirement income fund? The difference between the present value of the benefit package and the notional nest egg can be thought of as a *benefit gap* arising from CPP participation.

Finally, it is helpful to put participants from different eras on a comparable scale, since productivity growth and inflation make it otherwise difficult to compare the dollar amounts of 1976 with the dollar amounts of a century later. One way of doing this is to express the benefit gap as a percentage of covered earnings in the year each representative participant turns 65 (see Box 2 for a concrete example). Figure 2 shows benefit gaps for a set of such participants, using economic assumptions similar to those in the chief actuary's projections — most importantly, that nominal investment returns will average 6.0 percent (roughly 2.5 percent real returns plus an allowance for 3.5 percent inflation) over the projection period.

CPP participants with life profiles similar to those of our composite representative who had already retired by 1996 expe-

---

10 In the case of past contributions and notional interest, actual returns on the provincial securities held in the CPP account can be used; going forward, a variety of interest rate assumptions is possible.

Box 2: *Calculating the Benefit Gap*

To make the method of calculating benefit gaps from CPP participation concrete, let us examine the projected experience of an average participant born in 1996.

Following the life profile used throughout this paper, this participant enters the CPP at age 23 in 2019. He or she earns at or above the YMPE each year, pays CPP premiums according to the default rate schedule until age 62, and then draws disability benefits for three years. (In these simulations, disability benefits are treated as negative contributions in order to simplify the comparison of each participant's situation at age 65 — a treatment that lowers the amount of both the notional nest egg and the theoretical value of the benefits package but does not affect the crucial measure: the difference between them.)

Suppose that the 6 percent rate of return (roughly 2.5 percent real) projected by the chief actuary (Canada 1995) prevails over this composite participant's working lifetime. By the time he or she turns 65 at the beginning of 2061, a similar pattern of contributions and withdrawals into and out of a funded plan would have built up a retirement fund of just under $3.4 million, which is some six times the YMPE of $582,600 projected for 2061 (a little inflation goes a long way!).

The benefit package offered our participant by the CPP consists of a little more than 21.5 years of retirement benefits (based on projected life expectancy of this cohort at age 65), followed by a death benefit and five years of survivor benefits to a spouse after that. The present value of this package at the moment he or she turns 65 would, using the same 6 percent interest rate, be some $2.5 million, four and a half times the YMPE in 2061. Since the present value of the benefit package falls short of the notional nest egg by some $0.9 million — one and a half times the YMPE in 2061 — this representative participant has a negative benefit gap equal to one and a half years of covered earnings at age 65.

Suppose, alternatively, that returns average two percentage points higher over this composite participant's working lifetime — 8 percent or roughly 4.5 percent real. In that case, the same pattern of contributions and withdrawals to and from a funded plan would yield a retirement nest egg of some $5.5 million, which is nearly ten times the YMPE projected for 2061. The benefit package would, in the higher interest rate environment, cost a little more than $2 million, or more than three and a half times the YMPE. The difference of $3.5 million is more than six times the projected YMPE in 2061 — a loss from CPP participation equal to more than six years of covered earnings at age 65.

Figure 2: *CPP Benefit Gaps by Age,*
Assuming 6 Percent Nominal Returns

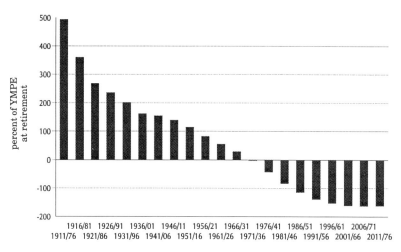

year of birth/retirement

rienced benefit gaps that were large and positive. Relative to what might have been achieved by using the same contributions to purchase benefits outside the CPP, such participants got a bonus equal to 200 percent or more of YMPE at age 65 — a gift of several years of covered earnings.[11] Later participants will not do so well. If the chief actuary's 2.5 percent real return comes to pass, today's ten-year-old who earns the YMPE or better over a working life and triggers a typical set of CPP benefits will lose the equivalent of just over one year's worth of covered earnings at age 65. For today's and tomorrow's toddlers, the situation is worse: participation in an unreformed CPP will cost them more than one and a half years' earnings.

In one key respect, however, this scenario may be considered relatively rosy. The attractiveness of a Ponzi game depends strongly

---

11 As explained in footnote 9, the presentation slightly exaggerates the benefit gaps experienced by the earliest cohorts

Figure 3: *CPP Benefit Gaps by Age,*
Assuming 8 Percent Nominal Returns

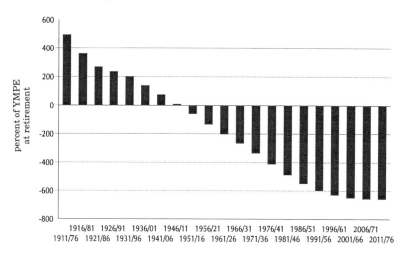

year of birth/retirement

on the returns that are available on alternative investments. The benefit gaps just calculated were based on a prevailing nominal rate of return of 6.0 percent. Real interest rates, however, are now considerably higher than those used in the chief actuary's projections: the gap between yields on long-term bonds and the year-over-year increase in the consumer price index (CPI) is almost six percentage points, and the yield on the federal government's real return bond stands around 4.2 percent. The results of calculating benefit gaps using an 8.0 percent nominal interest rate — about 4.5 percent in real terms — are staggering, as Figure 3 illustrates.

The representative participant who is ten years old today stands to lose the equivalent of five and a half years of covered earnings at age 65 by participating in an unreformed CPP. Today's and tomorrow's toddlers face an even worse deal: a negative benefit gap equal to six to six and a half years of covered earnings at age 65.

Morally Insupportable,
Politically Unsustainable

This situation is more than embarrassing: it is unconscionable. It is also, on the face of it, somewhat ridiculous. If the projections underlying Figure 3 — in particular, 4.5 percent real interest rates in the future — are borne out, the benefit gap of most Canadian workers of today and the future is strongly negative. A dispassionate observer who weighed the welfare of all participants equally would conclude that, on balance, the Ponzi game should end — that present and future Canadians considered together would be better off if the CPP simply ceased to exist.

The question of the CPP's sustainability is more complicated, however, since those currently of voting age can always choose to try to coerce those who will come after them into the scheme. And because the age at which Canadians enter the CPP generally follows quite closely the age at which they become eligible to vote, most voters have already seen some of their funds disappear into the scheme and have therefore begun to develop an interest in preserving it long enough to get their benefits.

Suppose, for example, that in 2001 a vote were held on whether the CPP should be wound up. As of the following year, the proposal would say, no more contributions would be collected and no new benefits would commence. Benefits already being paid would continue to be paid but from the regular federal budget — financed by, say, a higher goods and services tax (GST) rate.[12]

Although this example is crude in that it involves canceling accrued entitlements and glosses over some significant questions

---

12 The GST rate necessary to meet all currently projected benefits in 2001 would initially be about eight percentage points. This amount could be lower by, say, two percentage points if the then-existing balance in the CPP account were amortized over a ten-year period and could be lower still if benefits other than retirement benefits were not paid in full. The attraction of using consumption taxes to meet existing obligations under any windup scenario is that such taxes would allow some of the costs of those obligations to fall on those who benefited from the small contributions required in the CPP's early days.

Figure 4: *Effect on the Benefit Gap of*
Winding Up the CPP in 2001, by Age

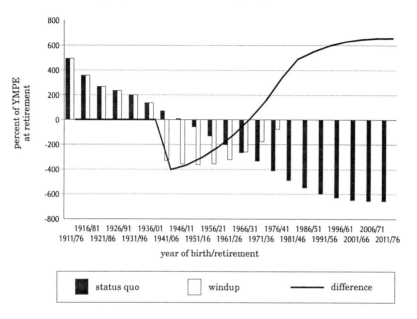

about covering benefits already being paid,[13] it captures key features of most plausible windup scenarios and allows a snapshot of the calculation that each age cohort would face. Figure 4 illustrates the impact by cohort, contrasting each age group's benefit gap under the windup scenario with the gap under the

---

13 Windup schemes that would simply stop payments to current retirees without compensation are conceivable. The disruptions they would cause to people too far advanced in life to adjust would, however, make them difficult to justify except in extreme circumstances. Not coincidentally, they would be difficult to legislate. The windup illustrated here would not stop such payments; indeed, it is incomplete in that it takes no explicit account of their financing. A political strategy for reform would probably involve initial financing of at least part of these benefits with deficits in the regular federal and/or provincial budgets, leaving part of the burden on future generations in the first instance, with further adjustments toward intergenerational fairness being made in regular government budgets during later years. See Townley (1981) for a formal discussion of this point.

Figure 5:   *Weighted Effect on the Benefit Gap of*
Winding Up the CPP in 2001, by Age [a]

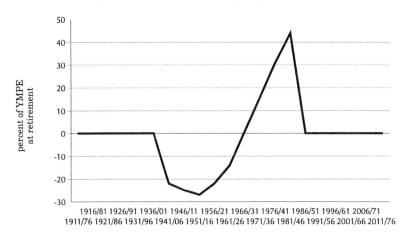

year of birth/retirement

[a]   Age weighted by share of voting-age population.

status quo. In short, cohorts already retired would be unaffected,
those on the verge of retirement would be major losers, and those
born after the late 1960s would, on average, come out ahead.

The problem from the point of view of today's and tomorrow's
toddlers is that they, the biggest winners from doing away with
a plan tilted badly against them, would not yet be voting in 2001.
The relatively numerous baby boomers, on the other hand, would
be big losers. The median voter would reject this plan. And when
the impact of windup on benefit gaps (the solid line in Figure 4)
is weighted by the proportion of each group in the voting age
population, as in Figure 5, the net impact across all participants
of windup is negative.

These calculations are highly stylized, of course, and omit
several considerations.[14] One is the possibility that concern over

_14_ Among them are the interactions of the CPP with other government programs. In the case of any windup of the plan, the then-existing configuration...

the lot of those not yet old enough to vote would motivate some older Canadians to vote against their self-interest. Currently, however, this possibility seems unlikely. Those urging CPP reform are repeatedly confronted with the unwillingness of many of those older Canadians who have done very well from the plan to even consider what a bad deal it is for the young. For this reason, a vote to windup the CPP in 2001 would be unlikely to carry.

What about a similar proposal put to the population in 2006? By then, five more years' worth of big losers under the CPP would have reached voting age. In addition, five more years' worth of older Canadians would have moved into a situation in which a CPP windup would affect them marginally or not at all (either because they were now receiving benefits or because they had passed beyond the reach of any fiscal measures). Against these considerations, the baby boomers would have paid into the CPP for five more years, increasing their interest in propping the system up until they see some return. On balance, however, the weighted benefit gap would be closer to favoring the windup scenario than was the case in 2001. Median voter calculations also suggest a move toward windup, but not far enough to achieve it, in 2006.

The further ahead one looks, however, the more the balance in favor of maintaining the system erodes. Over time, the negative impact of windup on the baby boomers rises as their contributions move into the past and their payouts approach, but their numbers shrink. By contrast, the ranks of the young, who would benefit from windup, swell. As Figure 6 illustrates, the balance of gains and losses gradually shifts. When benefit gaps are

Note 14 - cont'd.

...of other programs for the elderly and of income taxes generally would be important. For many individuals facing the high implicit marginal tax rates of the new elderly benefit, the loss of CPP benefits would be less traumatic than is pictured here; on the other hand, without the CPP, expenditure on the elderly benefit would go up, raising the issue of who would be taxed to pay for the increase.

Figure 6:   *Weighted Effect on the Benefit Gap of Winding Up the CPP in 2001, by Age* [a]

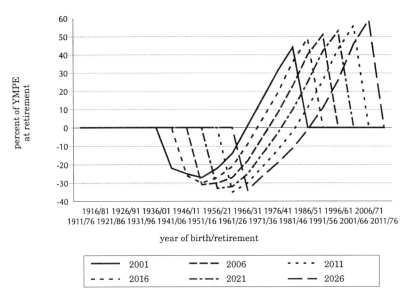

year of birth/retirement

——— 2001	— — — 2006	· · · · 2011
- - - · 2016	—·—· 2021	— — 2026

[a]   Age weighted by share of voting-age population.

summed across all cohorts — an approach that amounts to assuming that voting is affected by intensity of preference — that balance tips over in favor of getting rid of the CPP by 2011. Median voter calculations, in which intensity of preference does not matter, suggest that the tipover comes later, just before 2021 (Figure 7).

One cannot, of course, produce a precise prediction of the date of the CPP's collapse by looking at a calculation based on stylized participants whose votes explicitly depend on their net gains or losses from participation in the plan.[15] For one thing, if

15 Such simplified aggregations necessarily suppress details that may turn out to be important. One variable highlighted by Townley (1981) is the difference between the age at which people become eligible to vote and the age at which they enter the workforce. Recent trends toward later workforce entry are ominous for the CPP's survival since they are producing a growing bloc of voters who have not yet developed a vested interest in the plan's survival.

Figure 7: *Balance of Opinion Favoring*
Winding Up the CPP in Various Years

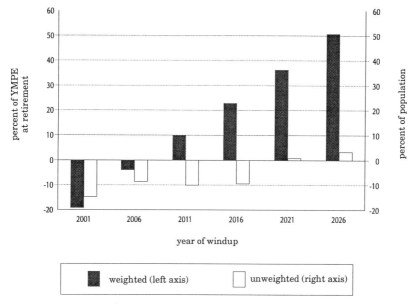

Note: Weighted balances are proportions of voters weighted by the size of their benefit
gaps; unweighted balances are proportions of gainers and losers with (as in
median-voter models) no account taken of intensity of preference. Age groups whose
benefit gaps are affected by less than the equivalent of three months' covered
earnings are assumed to be indifferent to the change.

the coalition in favor of winding up the plan was growing and
looked likely to become dominant, as would happen in my scenario well before the 2011–21 period, the increasing sense that
money put into the plan was money thrown away would prompt
demands for a quicker windup. Suppose, for example, that voters
in 2016 expected that, even if they voted to continue the plan, a
similar vote in 2021 would wind it up. Faced with an effective
choice between winding the CPP up in five years and winding it
up immediately, an overwhelming majority would vote for quick
action; the only nay voters would be those who would reach
eligibility for retirement benefits during the 2016–21 period.
Similarly, voters in 2011 who could anticipate the choice that

would face voters in 2016 would vote for an immediate windup — and so on, bringing the ultimate event forward in time. A dawning realization that the future does, in fact, hold such choices may be responsible for the fact that a debate over CPP reform is already occurring, even at a time when the vested interest of the majority of participants appears to favor continuing the plan unchanged.

In any event, the lesson is clear in a qualitative sense. Like all Ponzi games, the CPP requires new participants to fund the benefits of their predecessors. If alternatives are more attractive, as in a world of 4.5 percent real returns, the plan's sustainability cannot be taken for granted.

Those on the wrong end of big negative benefit gaps may, of course, look kindly on the CPP, as many of its current defenders do, *because* of its redistributive features, accepting the predominance of redistribution from the young to the old as integral to its design. Canada has a basic income support tier of benefits for the elderly, however, and numerous welfare and in-kind benefits to guard against destitution, as well as a steeply graduated personal income tax to fund them. The CPP looks and sounds like an income replacement program, providing benefits similar to those available from private pension plans and insurance policies — except that it is tilted dramatically against those who were unable to vote when it was established.

Moreover, tomorrow's older generation, unlike today's, will consist of people who never experienced the phenomenal returns that the CPP paid out to its first beneficiaries and whose willingness to face the truth about its impact on the young will be correspondingly greater. On balance, those politicians who promise to overturn an unreformed CPP — and there will be many of them in the twenty-first century — will likely get an increasingly enthusiastic response.

Options for Reform and Replacement

Recognition that the CPP's unfairness to the young threatens its sustainability over the long run — and to the extent that fears of future unsustainability are reflected in discontent over current contributions, its ability to survive in the shorter run as well — has prompted several suggestions for reforms to lessen the imbalance. Among the possibilities most often canvassed and figuring prominently in the governmental discussion paper are increases in the contribution rate to a level sufficient to keep the CPP account positive indefinitely without further increases and a scaling back of benefits (Governments of Canada 1996, 27–29; see also Robson 1996, 15–19; McCrossan 1995, 17–18). Less often mentioned but likely to command greater attention as time goes by are staged windups and the possibility of opting out by specific provinces.

Increasing Contributions and Trimming Benefits

A ten-year increase in CPP contribution rates to a level that could be sustained indefinitely would shave something off the costs that the plan threatens to impose on today's children and tomorrow's newborns. A quick move to higher rates would build up the CPP account; workers now nearing retirement but still paying CPP premiums would cover more of their own future benefits, shrinking the negative benefit gap today's youngsters face.

If real returns average 4.5 percent in the future, an 11.9 percent contribution rate if moved to in equal increments over a ten-year period would be sufficient to keep the CPP account positive indefinitely.[16] By comparison with the default contribution schedule, an 11.9 percent premium would worsen the benefit gaps of the representative CPP participants born before the early 1980s but improve the situation of those who come after them. Figure 8 compares the benefit gaps facing representative participants under the two regimes. Moving to an 11.9 percent contri-

---

16 The discussion paper thus calls this a "steady-state contribution rate" (Governments of Canada 1996, 27–29). The rates its authors use differ from those used here, however, because of different interest rate assumptions.

Figure 8: *Benefit Gaps by Age under the Default*
Contribution Schedule and an Increased-Rate Alternative

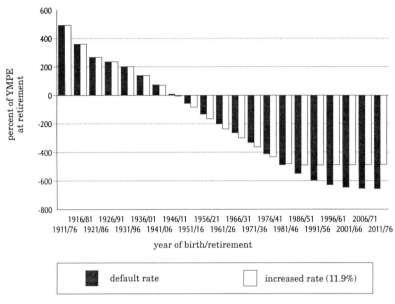

Note: All the calculations assume an 8.0 percent nominal (4.5 percent real) rate of return.
The increased-rate calculations assume moving to an 11.9 percent contribution rate
in equal increments over ten years, starting in 1997.

bution rate over ten years would reduce the negative benefit gap
for those born after 1980 to the equivalent of just under five years'
covered earnings at age 65.

Another possibility is to scale back CPP benefits. The governmental discussion paper (Governments of Canada 1996, 29,
33–43) discusses the possibility of scaling benefit costs back by
10 percent. Assuming 4.5 percent real returns over the long haul,
such a cut over a ten-year period would lower the contribution
rate needed to keep the CPP account positive indefinitely from
11.9 to 10.7 percent. Figure 9 compares the benefit gaps facing
representative participants of various ages under three regimes:
the current benefit structure and the default rate structure; the
current benefit structure and an 11.9 percent contribution rate;

Figure 9: *Benefit Gaps by Age under the Default*
Contribution Schedule and Increased-Rate
and Benefit-Cut Alternatives

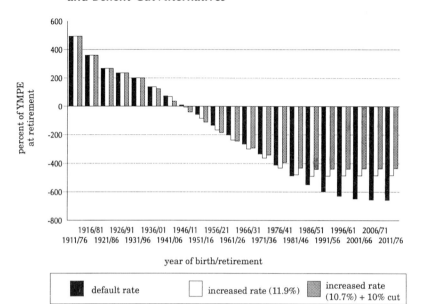

Note: All the calculations assume an 8.0 percent nominal (4.5 percent real) rate of return.
The calculations involving rate increases and benefit cuts assume making these
changes in equal increments over ten years.

and the scaled-back benefit structure with the corresponding
lower contribution rate of 10.7 percent. With pared-back benefits
lowering the overall investment required in the plan, the penalty
exacted by CPP participation on cohorts born from the early
1980s forward would fall to a little less than four and a half years'
worth of covered earnings at age 65.

The combined impact of a flat rate and pared-back benefits
would improve the picture dramatically relative to the current
situation, in which tomorrow's toddlers are faced with a negative
benefit gap of more than six years' covered earnings at age 65. I
undertook an exercise, similar to the one earlier, examining the
impact of windup on various age cohorts. It is not shown here, but
it reveals that such a package of reforms would postpone the day

when self-interested voters would vote to wind the plan up until after 2030 — at which point demographic uncertainties make this sort of exercise even more speculative.

More Radical Reforms

Such changes would mean that the bulk of today's CPP participants would have less advantageous benefit gaps than they had previously expected. The same changes would also trigger a buildup of funds in the CPP account that would, once the new higher rate was reached, reach vast proportions; given a contribution rate of 10.7 percent and benefits scaled back by 10 percent, the balance in the account would surpass $100 billion in 2007 and $200 billion in 2012. A number of new avenues of debate would open as a result.

Some Canadians, preferring the terms that the Ponzi game had previously offered them, would launch a fresh effort for richer benefits, citing the buildup of funds in the CPP account as evidence of affordability. Others, faced with a truer accounting of the plan's long-run impact on younger participants, would more vigorously challenge the fairness of continuing with even a slimmed-down plan. Still others would urge that the money accumulating in the account be earmarked for individual participants or put under their direct control, in order to protect it from government mismanagement and enhance the beneficial effects that this addition to national saving would likely have on future investment and growth. The possibility of a tug-of-war, with a move back to better benefit gaps for early baby boomers followed by a vote to wind up the plan a decade later, cannot be overlooked.

If problems associated with raising rates, trimming benefits, and managing a pool of investable funds prove too difficult for the CPP's cumbersome amending formula to deal with, another avenue for radical reform may appear attractive. In response to general concerns about the invasion of provincial jurisdiction over pensions and to Quebec's specific desire to set up its own pension

Figure 10: *Median Age and Net Debt per Person, by Province*

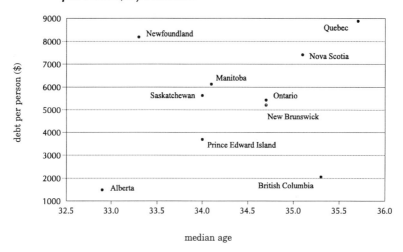

median age

Source: Statistics Canada, CANSIM database on CD-ROM.

Note: Debt figures, which are consolidated provincial and local net debt on a Financial Management System basis, are for 1993. Median age is for 1995.

plan, the *Canada Pension Plan Act* has included, from its inception, a provision for provinces to opt out and establish their own universal plans. Although no province except Quebec has acted on this possibility or even discussed it much recently, the intensified debate about the CPP that is likely in coming years may awaken such notions in provinces whose demographics are relatively favorable and whose revealed preferences in fiscal policy generally suggest an aversion to imposing large burdens on the young.

Figure 10 graphs the provinces' median age and net debt per person, two possibly useful indicators of the extent to which a separate plan involving more radical reforms might be attractive. Other things being equal, one might expect relatively young and fiscally conservative provinces — Alberta being the standout — to be more favorably disposed to independent reform.[17] If one

17 Although Quebec has its own pension plan, it is included in the graph for comparison and because its vote counts in considering amendments to the...

province, especially a young and wealthy one, were to opt out, others would naturally contemplate doing likewise.

Though radical by comparison with the inertia that has characterized this policy area in the past, provincialization would be a logical response by certain provinces to paralysis or inadequate reform of the CPP.

Sending Ponzi Packing

The thrust of this discussion is straightforward. As all Ponzi schemes eventually must, the CPP is losing its ability to draw new participants in willingly. Increased coercion applied to the young, who would be much better off outside the system, is no long-term solution. No benefit reductions and a slow move to higher rates, as under the default contribution schedule, will mean higher ultimate rates and horrendous benefit gaps for today's youngsters, making the emergence of a coalition powerful enough to overturn the plan only a matter of time. But quicker moves on both fronts will raise doubts about the plan's survival in the shorter term. The 20-year-old asking why CPP contributions have roughly doubled while benefits are being cut is not likely to be satisfied by the answer, "So that your kids can lose four and a half years' worth of earnings rather than six and a half!"

For this reason, it makes sense for Canadians to expand the debate about the future of income replacement programs for the elderly beyond contribution hikes and minor benefit trimming. Although official recognition of the CPP's unfairness to the young is welcome, the assumption that coercing unwilling participants into the Ponzi scheme is a viable option over the long haul is unwarranted. Ultimately, the accumulating evidence of govern-

---

Note 17 - cont'd.

...CPP. It is worth noting, in passing, that the province's population was relatively much younger in 1966, when the Quebec Pension Plan was set up, than it is now.

ments' inability to run income replacement programs for the old in a manner that is fair to the young may lead Canadians, like citizens of many other countries, to re-evaluate the state's role in this area and opt to phase out the CPP in favor of expanded private retirement saving.[18] It would be wise to prepare for that eventuality not only by improving the CPP's financial condition with fuller funding but by trimming it back and simultaneously improving the tax and regulatory treatment of private pension and registered retirement savings plans.

In thinking about these alternatives, it is always necessary to keep in mind that Canada is approaching the late stages of the Ponzi game, in which the recruitment of new participants whose funds will pay the benefits of those about to start receiving is becoming more difficult and may ultimately prove impossible. Rhetoric about "risk-free" and "guaranteed" benefits from the CPP is unhelpful; the plan is too unfair and too exposed to political risks to guarantee anything. It is irresponsible of today's adults to try to impose the CPP on today's children and unrealistic to think that, when those children reach adulthood, they will accept the attempt if it is made. Canadians need to start preparing for a future without the CPP.

---

18 The World Bank (1994) provides a sobering survey of mismanagement of public sector income replacement schemes around the world. For an outline of steps that would allow the CPP to be wound up without major disruption, see Robson (1996, 20–22).

References

Canada. 1995. Office of the Superintendent of Financial Institutions. *Canada Pension Plan: Fifteenth Actuarial Report as at 31 December 1993*. Ottawa.

Deeson, A.F.L. 1971. *Great Swindlers*. London: W. Foulsham.

Federal, Provincial, and Territorial Governments of Canada (Governments of Canada). 1996. *An Information Paper for Consultations on the Canada Pension Plan*. Ottawa: Department of Finance.

Grant, Michael. 1996. *Ponzi Game Up? Canadian Youth and the Canada Pension Plan Reforms*. Ottawa: Canadian Youth Foundation.

McCrossan, Paul. 1995. "Replacing the Canada Pension Plan: The Problems of Transition." Paper presented to the Fraser Institute conference, Replacing the Canada Pension Plan. November 15.

Robson, William B.P. 1996. *Putting Some Gold in the Golden Years: Reforming the Canada Pension Plan*. C.D. Howe Institute Commentary 76. Toronto: C.D. Howe Institute, January.

Samuelson, Paul A. 1967. "Social Security." *Newsweek*, February 13, p. 88.

Townley, Peter. 1981. "Public Choice and the Social Insurance Paradox: A Note." *Canadian Journal of Economics* 14 (November): 712–717.

World Bank. 1994. *Averting the Old Age Crisis: Policies to Protect the Old and Promote Growth*. New York: Oxford University Press.

A Case for Abolishing
Tax-Deferred Saving Plans

Christopher Ragan

In 1957, the Canadian government introduced registered retirement saving plans (RRSPs), permitting individuals to make deposits into saving plans that receive special tax advantages. Similar tax advantages were already available to some individuals through firm-sponsored pension plans or public service superannuation plans, both of which are referred to as registered pension plans (RPPs). Contributions to RRSPs and RPPs are tax deductible in the year they are made; the funds accumulate within the plan without taxation of interest or dividend income but are taxed as regular income when they are withdrawn.

The benefit to individual contributors from such tax-deferred saving plans (TDSPs) is reflected by the very significant growth in annual contributions since their inception. Figure 1 shows the annual flow of contributions, measured in constant 1992 dollars, into RRSPs and RPPs since 1960. RPPs were far more important than RRSPs in the early 1960s, which is not surprising given that RRSPs had been created only a few years earlier. Individuals contributed $27.7 million into RRSPs in 1960 but more than $330 million to RPPs in the same year. By 1970, RRSPs had become relatively more important but were still dominated by RPPs; in that year, individuals put $225 million into RRSPs and almost $730 million to RPPs. But in 1976, annual contributions

I thank, without implicating, Hubert Frenken, Seamus Hogan, John Richards, Bill Robson, and Bill Watson for helpful comments. Any remaining errors are mine.

Figure 1:   *Annual Contributions to RRSPs and RPPs, 1960–92* [a]

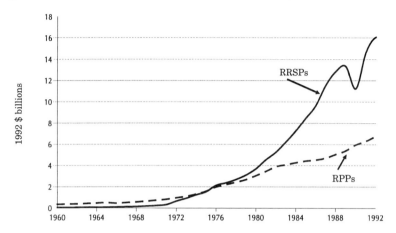

[a] Employers' contributions to RPPs not included.

Source: Canada, Department of National Revenue, *Taxation Statistics*, various years.

to RRSPs overtook those to RPPs, and the gap has increased dramatically since then. By 1992, the annual flow of contributions to RRSPs totaled just over $16 billion, whereas only $6.7 billion was being contributed to RPPs. Clearly, RRSPs have evolved to the point where today the annual contributions represent an enormous sum of money.

The growth of RRSPs as a vehicle of individual saving probably reflects two factors: increased public awareness of the existence of RRSPs and their increased generosity. (The two are unlikely to be independent of each other.) Table 1 shows the evolution of RRSP contribution limits since the inception of the plans. Their generosity rose dramatically in 1972, when the maximum contribution increased from 10 percent of earned income to 20 percent. Since that time, however, the adjustments have mostly been increases in the nominal contribution limit to reflect increases in the overall price level. An important change in the RRSP program, which took place in 1991, was an attempt to better harmonize the limits for individuals with and without

Table 1:   RRSP Contribution Limits, 1957–94

Year of Policy Change	Individuals without RPPs	Individuals with RPPs
1957	10% of earned income to a maximum of $2,500	10% of earned income to a maximum of $1,500
1972	20% of earned income to a maximum of $4,000	20% of earned income to a maximum of $2,500
1976	20% of earned income to a maximum of $5,500	20% of earned income to a maximum of $2,500
1986	20% of earned income to a maximum of $7,500	20% of earned income to a maximum of $3,500
1991	18% of earned income to a maximum of $11,500	18% of earned income to a maximum of $11,500 – PA[a]
1993	18% of earned income to a maximum of $12,500	18% of earned income to a maximum of $12,500 – PA[a]
1994	18% of earned income to a maximum of $13,500	18% of earned income to a maximum of $13,500 – PA[a]
1996[b]	planned freeze of limit until 2003	

[a] PA is the individual's pension adjustment, which reflects benefits from an employer-sponsored RPP. For individuals with a defined-contribution plan, PA is the sum of the employer and employee contributions. For a defined-benefit plan, PA is computed with an imputation based on the details of the plan. See Horner and Poddar (1992).

[b] Announced in the 1996 federal budget.

employer-sponsored pension plans; it was accomplished by introducing the concept of the pension adjustment (PA).[1]

Recent attention in the press and elsewhere has tended to focus on the importance of RRSPs, ignoring the existence of other TDSPs, especially firm-sponsored pension plans and public service superannuation plans. But RRSPs and employer-sponsored plans are essentially the same type of saving vehicle, so any analysis of one should not ignore the other. Thus, throughout this study, I refer to *all* tax-deferred saving plans as TDSPs.

[1] See Horner and Poddar (1992) for a clear discussion of the PA.

The Plan of the Paper. In this paper, I argue for eliminating all TDSPs on the grounds that they impose greater costs on society than they confer in benefits. I do not ignore the fact that individual contributors certainly benefit from TDSPs, but I argue that these benefits exist only by imposing costs on noncontributors. I also argue that this implicit redistribution of income is contrary to the overall goals of the tax-and-transfer system — that is, income is redistributed away from lower-income earners toward higher-income earners.

The next section presents a number of alleged benefits of TDSPs and the reasons these benefits are largely illusory. I then address the specific costs associated with TDSPs, emphasizing their undesirable effects on the overall distribution of income. Next I sketch a package of complementary policy proposals, designed to be implemented together with my main proposal of abolishing TDSPs. The following section sets out an important caveat: that the desirability of eliminating TDSPs should be examined completely separately from its effect on the government budget deficit — in other words, that such a move should not be motivated by a desire to increase government tax revenues. The last section contains my final comments.

Alleged Benefits of TDSPs

TDSPs are often said to have three benefits: they increase the level of national saving; they are a desirable part of income tax reform in that they are a move toward a consumption-based tax system; and they reduce the need for government-provided income support programs. Each of these claims deserves consideration.

Increased National Saving

National saving is defined as the sum of household, corporate, and government saving. Each component can be positive or negative. In 1994, for example, household and corporate savings were equal to 5.3 percent and 2.7 percent of gross national product (GNP), respectively; in contrast, saving by all levels of government combined equaled – 4.5 percent of GNP. This negative saving simply reflects the large fiscal deficits at that time. Overall, national saving was 3.5 percent of GNP in 1994.

In Canada and even more in the United States, low national saving rates have been a concern in recent years. The low rates in North America are contrasted with the much higher rates in the Asian tigers, countries that have experienced rates of real economic growth over the past three decades significantly higher than those of Canada and the United States. This concern about low national saving rates seems to be driven by the fear that a low level of domestic saving necessarily implies a low rate of domestic capital formation and, as a result, a lower future rate of real economic growth.

Two quite separate issues have to be addressed when examining the proposition that TDSPs should be used as a policy instrument to promote national saving. The first concerns why a government might want to take specific policy actions to promote domestic saving. The second relates to whether TDSPs are an effective instrument for bringing about an increase in national saving.

Should Government Actively Encourage Saving?

A country with higher domestic saving is unquestionably a country with higher future wealth. There may be some debate about the form that greater wealth will take, but there is no doubt that more saving leads to more wealth.

In a closed economy, an increase in saving resulting from a change in household or corporate behavior (perhaps in response to a change in government policy) must lead to an equal change in domestic investment, which, in turn, leads to a greater ability to produce and consume goods in the future. In an economy that is closely connected to world credit markets, however, increased domestic saving may simply leave the country and be used to acquire foreign assets, which will generate a return that permits domestic residents to consume more goods in the future. So, in either a closed or an open economy, an increase in saving leads to higher future wealth. The form of that wealth may be different — in a closed economy, it must be a larger domestic stock of physical capital, whereas in an open economy, it is likely to be a larger stock of domestically owned foreign assets — but in both cases there is more wealth.

Does this fact not immediately imply that saving is a good thing and that the government is justified in implementing policies to encourage saving? After all, is it not obvious that more future wealth is desirable? Unfortunately, the logic is not quite so simple. Note that the increase in future wealth does not come free. The price that must be paid is the sacrifice of current consumption and thus current well-being (not consuming is, after all, what saving is all about). One must therefore ask whether the benefits of higher future consumption necessarily outweigh the costs associated with lower current consumption. It is not obvious that a policy designed to encourage people to reduce their current consumption so that they (or their children) can enjoy greater future consumption actually succeeds in improving over-all well-being.

Probable Reduction in National Saving

For the purposes of this paper, however, the debate surrounding the benefits of higher domestic saving is really secondary to the debate over whether TDSPs can be an effective instrument for increasing national saving. Unfortunately, the relationship between TDSPs and national saving has received scant attention in the academic literature. What little research does exist tends to focus on the United States, and even then the emphasis is on the relationship between TDSPs and the level of household saving (see, for example, Venti and Wise 1990). In the absence of established empirical relationships, one is left to examine the theory of the likely relationship between TDSPs and national saving.

To examine the impact of TDSPs on national saving, it is necessary to understand how they separately affect household saving and government saving.

Household Saving. Household saving is equal to the difference between household income and household expenditure in a given period of time. (For what follows, think of an individual as representing the household.)

The empirical evidence suggests that an individual with access to a TDSP will almost certainly save more than an otherwise identical individual without such access (Venti and Wise 1990; 1994; Gale and Scholz 1994). In other words, TDSPs almost certainly increase household saving. From a theoretical perspective, this finding is not surprising. To see the logic, consider a simple example of two taxpayers, each of whom has a marginal income tax rate of 40 percent and annually saves $5,000 of current income. If one now reduces his non-TDSP saving by $5,000 in order to make a $5,000 contribution to a TDSP — thereby leaving his total saving unchanged — then his current taxable income is reduced by $5,000 and the income tax bill on it by $2,000. As long as this individual saves some part of his increase in current disposable income, his total saving will be higher than that of the other taxpayer who does not use a TDSP. Most economists would predict that the individual who is richer by $2,000 in disposable income will spend some of it and save the rest. It seems reasonable to expect that people will increase both their current expenditure and their current saving as a result of the increase in disposable income.[2]

---

2 Note that this result requires only the income effect generated by the TDSP contribution. If both current and future consumption are normal goods (goods that people demand more of when income rises), then the increase in wealth produced by the TDSP contribution will lead to higher current consumption and higher current saving. The substitution effect of a TDSP is examined in the next section.

Government Saving. Government saving is the excess of a government's revenue over its expenditures. (A government budget deficit thus implies negative government saving, or what is often called *dissaving*.)

Even if TDSPs do lead to an increase in household saving, they almost certainly reduce the level of government saving. When individuals who contribute to TDSPs experience a reduction in their current income tax obligations, as in the example above, the government experiences an equal reduction in current income tax revenue. For any given level of government expenditure, this reduction in tax revenue implies a reduction in the level of government saving or, if it is already running a budget deficit, an increase in its level of dissaving.[3]

To illustrate the magnitude of the effect of TDSPs on government tax revenue, Table 2 shows the reduction in the federal government's personal income tax revenues that is attributed to RRSPs and RPPs for 1991 and 1992. The computation of the loss in tax revenue has three parts: the tax revenue lost from the flow of funds into TDSPs; the tax revenue lost from the fact that the stock of funds within the TDSPs generates interest income that is not taxed; and finally, the increase in tax revenue when funds are withdrawn from TDSPs. The combined loss in personal income tax revenue to the federal government from RRSPs and RPPs in 1992 was $13.6 billion. Given the current federal-provincial split in personal income tax revenues, a reasonable guess of the loss to the two levels of government combined might be about $20 billion for that year.[4]

---

3 Note that the reduction in government tax revenue implies a reduction in government saving for a *given* level of government expenditure. For analytical purposes, it is useful to distinguish the changes in government saving that come about from the TDSP-induced reduction in revenues from those that come about from any possible reduction in government spending.

4 The size of this revenue loss will vary over time. The numbers in Table 2 represent the tax revenue losses associated with a system of TDSPs that are immature in the sense that they have not been in place, in their current form and with current limits, for a long period of time. Eventually, if the population and real per capita income were constant, the annual flow of contributions...

Table 2: *Federal Personal Income Tax Expenditures from RRSPs and RPPs, 1991 and 1992*

	1991	1992
	($ billions)	
Registered retirement saving plans		
Deductions for contributions	3.310	3.685
Nontaxation of investment income	2.980	2.755
Taxation of withdrawals	– 0.925	– 0.940
Total revenue loss from RRSPs	*5.365*	*5.500*
Registered pension plans		
Deductions for contributions	4.460	4.990
Nontaxation of investment income	8.950	7.690
Taxation of withdrawals	– 4.030	– 4.580
Total revenue loss from RPPs	*9.380*	*8.100*

Source: Canada 1994.

National Saving. If TDSPs lead to a rise in household saving but a fall in government saving, the overall effect on national saving is simply the difference between national income and total national expenditure. As just explained, individuals are likely to increase their spending as a result of the increase in disposable income generated by their TDSP contributions. Thus, unless the government reduces its level of expenditure by more than the increase in private expenditure, national saving will certainly

---

Note 4 - cont'd.

...would approximately equal the annual flow of withdrawals, leaving the untaxed income generated within the TDSPs as the main source of tax revenue loss. With the population and per capita income growing, however, the flow of contributions (made by young people) will tend to be larger than the flow of withdrawals (made by older people). Thus, the first row in each part of Table 2 will continue to exceed the third row. Moreover, the stock of funds within the TDSPs will continue to grow, implying an ever-increasing revenue loss from the untaxed capital income.

fall. Under the economist's standard analytical assumption of *ceteris paribus* — holding all other things (such as government spending) constant — the overall effect of TDSPs is therefore likely to be an increase in aggregate expenditure and a decrease in national saving.

A Shred of Evidence. Gale and Scholz (1994) provide some US evidence in support of this overall effect of TDSPs on national saving. They examine the effects on saving from increasing the annual contribution limits to individual retirement accounts (IRAs), which are US saving instruments similar to RRSPs. Stressing the importance of the fraction of the accompanying tax cut that individuals save, Gale and Scholz conclude that, if taxpayers were to save all of the tax cut, only 2 percent of the increased IRA contributions would represent a net addition to national saving.[5] Under the more likely assumption that individuals would save only half of the tax cut, the authors conclude that the increased IRA contributions would be associated with a reduction in national saving.

Similar empirical evidence for Canada does not yet exist in published form. However, research currently under way in which I am involved, based on Statistics Canada's 1992 Survey of Family Expenditure and using Gale and Scholz's basic approach, suggests results similar to those obtained in the United States. An increase in the RRSP limits leads to an increase in household saving and a larger reduction in government saving for a net result of an overall reduction in national saving. The implication is that the complete elimination of RRSPs would *reduce* household saving but would actually *increase* national saving.

---

5 If individuals saved all of the tax cut and national saving still rose (if only by a little), government spending must fall (slightly) in response to the reduction in tax revenue.

A Move toward
a Consumption Tax

A second argument in support of TDSPs is that they can be used to transform an income tax system into a consumption tax system, while still keeping in place the basic income tax structure. The main benefit of the switch is that income taxes distort the real return to saving. By taxing interest earnings, income taxes lower that return and thus, at the margin, discourage saving. In contrast, a consumption tax, such as the goods and services tax (GST), neither encourages nor discourages saving.

Since TDSPs permit individuals to defer taxable income from the year in which they earn it to the year in which they spend it, some people view such plans as a way to avoid the distortion caused by the taxation of interest income. To transform an income tax into a consumption tax, however, TDSPs must generate a substitution effect — a change in relative prices — that exactly offsets the distortion to the return to saving caused by the income tax. In other words, the introduction of TDSPs into a system that already taxes interest income must generate a substitution effect that increases saving.

This argument presents two problems: the substitution effect may not occur (or may be perverse); and only a minority of the population use TDSPs.

The Substitution Effect

The introduction of TDSPs may produce no substitution effect at all, an outcome that would be the case in a proportional income tax system in which all individuals made the maximum allowable contribution to a TDSP. Alternatively, TDSPs may generate a perverse substitution effect, as could happen in a system in which marginal tax rates rise with income. The implication is that introducing TDSPs to an income tax system may actually move it away from the desired goal of a consumption tax system.

The basic argument is as follows.[6] When TDSPs are introduced as an additional avenue of saving, individuals face a portfolio decision between two alternative saving instruments: tax-sheltered saving inside a TDSP and "normal" saving outside a TDSP. The wealth-maximizing portfolio is the one that equates the rates of return at the margin across the two types of saving. It follows that the interest rate that governs the individual's consumption-saving decision is the after-tax interest rate (which is the rate of return on "normal" saving). The implication is that TDSPs do not remove the distortion caused by the taxation of interest income, and thus they do not successfully transform an income tax system into a consumption tax system.[7]

Minority Use

Another reason — and a more commonsense one — why RRSPs may not be successful in converting an income-based tax into a consumption-based tax is that their use is optional, and, indeed, the data suggest that only a minority of the population use them. Data in Statistics Canada's Survey of Family Expenditure suggest that only about 30 percent of households were net contributors to RRSPs in 1992. For the majority of citizens who do not contribute to RRSPs, facing a consumption tax rather than an income tax is not an issue. It seems difficult to believe that the most effective way of transforming an income-based tax into a

---

6 I discuss this point in detail in Ragan (1994).

7 The possibility of a perverse substitution effect from TDSPs — one that exacerbates the distortion from the income tax — occurs in an income tax system with increasing marginal tax rates. The intertemporal redistribution of taxable income brought about by the TDSP contributions increases the individual's future taxable income and thereby his future marginal tax rate, effectively reducing the after-tax interest rate earned on "normal" saving. In this case, the introduction of the TDSP actually increases the existing distortion by generating a substitution effect that further reduces saving.

consumption-based tax is with an optional saving instrument that is used by only a minority of households.[8]

If TDSPs can not successfully transform the system into a consumption-based tax, it is not clear that they ought to be an integral part of general tax reform. The goal of moving toward a consumption-based system of taxation need not be abandoned, however. Rather than expanding the use or generosity of RRSPs, it would probably be far easier to diminish the importance of income taxes by reducing their rates at all income levels and, at the same time, increasing the role of consumption taxes, such as the GST. This shift would constitute a simple and successful move toward a system of consumption-based taxes. (I discuss this possibility more fully in a later section of the paper.)

Reduced Need for Income Support Programs

A third alleged benefit of TDSPs is that, by encouraging individuals to save more for retirement, such plans allow the government to spend fewer resources on retirement income support programs, such as old age security (OAS) and the guaranteed income supplement (GIS).[9] This view of TDSPs as a way of reducing the long-run demands on the public purse seems to have been an important motive behind recent reforms in Canada's pension rules (see, for example, Horner and Poddar 1992).

Two logically distinct questions arise. Is government justified in encouraging private saving for retirement? Are TDSPs the best way to attain this goal?

---

8 Of course, if all saving were required to be inside TDSPs, they would be successful in changing an income tax into a consumption tax. What reduces their ability to convert the tax system is that TDSPs are an alternative saving instrument. See Ragan (1994).

9 Both programs are scheduled to become part of the new seniors benefit in a few years.

Is Paternalism Appropriate?

Some people may argue that the government should not be so paternalistic as to tell people that they should save more than they are currently saving. Indeed, if Canadians, acting through their governments, were prepared to commit themselves to *not* providing financial assistance to those individuals deemed to be in need, then it would be reasonable for the government to have an entirely neutral policy — one that made no attempt either to encourage or to discourage private saving. But Canadians as a group apparently are committed to providing income support to low-income individuals. And given that commitment, it is entirely reasonable that the government, motivated by the scarcity of public funds, try to encourage individuals to save for their own retirement.

In the language of economists, the argument is essentially that the government's commitment to providing financial assistance to low-income people introduces an externality into people's saving behavior. Not saving enough during their working lives raises the chances that they will need government income assistance during retirement, which imposes costs on the rest of society. Thus, there is an argument for the government to encourage individuals to save more for their retirement.

The Saving-Incentive Problem

Given that the government has a reasonable justification for encouraging people to increase their own private saving and given that TDSPs almost certainly increase private saving, the main issue remaining is whether TDSPs are the best way to reduce the demands on the public purse. Is there an alternative policy tool that might be preferable?

An important practical problem with the government's commitment to retirement income support programs is that the generosity they embody may provide incentives for individuals not to save while they are working. Some fraction of the people who are legitimately deemed to need financial assistance during their retirement had moderate income streams during their working life. These individuals could have chosen to save more during their working years; instead, they chose to spend more, with the result that they command fewer resources during their retirement. By being committed to providing income support to these people, the government is essentially encouraging them not to save adequately during their working lives.

Given the government's long-standing commitment to providing income support where needed, the incentives to private saving contained in TDSPs may not be sufficient to induce low-income people to save enough so that they will not require government assistance when they are retired — a situation that can be called the "saving-incentive problem." Horner and Poddar (1992) suggest that precisely this effect is operating when they note, first, that the combined benefits from OAS, GIS, and the Canada and Quebec Pension Plans (CPP/QPP) drop sharply as income increases, and, second, that low-income earners tend to be seriously underrepresented among the individuals who make contributions to RRSPs.

RRSPs do not solve the saving-incentive problem largely because they are entirely voluntary. Low-income individuals can simply choose not to take advantage of RRSPs, thereby allowing a higher level of consumption during their working lives, while knowing that they will receive government assistance when retired.

If the primary motivation behind RRSPs is that government can thereby provide less income support to retired individuals, then a social security system with mandatory contributions may be more sensible. This is not to suggest that the current CPP/QPP programs do not have their problems (some of the other papers in this volume discuss these problems) or that they would be ideal systems even if those immediate problems were solved. The point is simply that *mandatory* pension plans completely avoid the saving-incentive problem; they constitute forced saving of the purest form. (I discuss this point again later in the paper.)

Some Costs of TDSPs

The three arguments in support of TDSPs do not present a strong case; there seems little reason to expect significant benefits from introducing TDSPs into an economy in which such plans are absent. It does not follow, however, that eliminating TDSPs would have significant benefits, given that they are already part of the Canadian income tax system. Any benefits from their elimination depend on the costs they are currently imposing. So I turn now to a discussion of two such costs, both relating to changes in the distribution of income.

Redistribution toward TDSP Contributors

Table 2 shows that RRSPs and RPPs together lead to significant reductions in income tax revenues. Faced with such a shortfall, the government must choose from the following four budgetary options.[10]

First, it can increase other current taxes to finance its current expenditures. If the specific tax increases fall only on those who benefit from making TDSP contributions, then the combination of the TDSP and tax increase will leave the distribution of income unchanged. But in general this coincidence will not occur. Some part of the burden of the tax increase will fall on individuals who do not benefit directly from a TDSP. In this case, there will be a redistribution of income associated with the TDSPs that should be recognized.

The second possibility is for the government to finance its expenditures by increasing its current level of borrowing — borrowing that ultimately must be financed by higher future taxes. Since any increase in future taxes almost certainly will fall

---

10 TDSPs obviously reduce income tax revenue for both federal and provincial governments. For simplicity, I group all levels of government together.

on some individuals who are not the current beneficiaries of TDSPs, this option has an associated intertemporal redistribution of income. The benefits to current TDSP contributors will be financed by taxes paid by future generations.

Third, the government can raise the required revenue by borrowing from the Bank of Canada. Such borrowing from the central bank will, however, have the effect of increasing the supply of money in circulation, with the eventual effect of a higher rate of inflation. Inflation imposes costs not only on those individuals whose incomes are not fully indexed but also on the economy as a whole as the efficiency of the price system is undermined. The former costs are largely a matter of income distribution; the latter are more an issue relevant to the real productive capacity of the economy.

Finally, the government that is experiencing a revenue shortfall can choose to reduce the level of its current expenditures so that no revenue increase is necessary. Before one can predict the effects of such cutbacks, it is important to know which expenditures will be reduced. But the general principle is the same as for the case of tax increases. If the expenditures that are eliminated would have benefited only those who receive direct benefits from TDSPs, the distribution of income will be unaffected. But as long as some of the now-eliminated expenditures would have benefited those who did not benefit from TDSPs, there will be a redistribution of income that should be recognized.

The general point here is simple: somebody pays. The tax advantages to TDSP contributors imply a significant loss of tax revenue for government. Such tax expenditures put considerable strain on public finances. Relief must come from other tax increases, from expenditure cuts, or from inflation; in all cases, the burden of the remedy cuts will probably not be distributed in the same manner as will the benefits from making contributions to TDSPs. Thus, TDSPs generate a redistribution away from non-contributors and toward contributors. Since the goals of income redistribution policy are usually cast in terms of redistributing according to income, the TDSP-induced redistribution may well be operating against current overall policy.

Redistribution in the Wrong Direction

Many elements of the tax-and-transfer system are designed to effect a redistribution of income away from high-income individuals toward lower-income individuals. Progressive income taxes involve such a redistribution, as do the GIS and OAS (both being financed out of general tax revenues). These redistribution schemes reflect a desire on the part of a majority of Canadians to offset, at least in part, some of the undesirable outcomes of a decentralized free market system while maintaining the benefits of the tremendous flexibility and incentive structures it contains.

Tax-deferred saving plans such as RRSPs and RPPs almost certainly redistribute income in the opposite direction, so they work at cross-purposes to the overall tax-and-transfer system. Two distinct redistributions are at work here. First, as just discussed, TDSPs bring about a redistribution of income away from noncontributors and toward contributors. To the extent that noncontributors tend to have lower incomes than contributors, this redistribution is going in the wrong direction. Second, the combination of the income tax structure and the TDSP contribution limits generates a redistribution of income away from low-income contributors and toward higher-income contributors.

Incomes of Contributors and Noncontributors

As I argued above, TDSPs generate a redistribution of income toward contributors and away from noncontributors. In other words, the significant benefits that accrue to contributors are paid for, in part, by people who for whatever reason do not take advantage of TDSPs.

Table 3 shows that in 1991 only 24 percent of those individuals who contributed to RRSPs had incomes of less than $20,000. Perhaps more striking is the fact that this group made only 14 percent of all RRSP contributions. In contrast, 12 percent of RRSP contributors had incomes in excess of $60,000 and these individuals made 24 percent of all that year's RRSP contributions. The gist of these data is repeated by statistics from another source for another recent year: the 1992 Survey of Family Expenditures reports that the mean disposable income of RRSP contributors was more than $50,000 whereas the mean for non-contributors was less than $30,000.

That noncontributors are more likely to have low incomes than are contributors is not surprising. After all, people with low incomes are not typically characterized as active savers; they usually feel unable to set aside significant sums for their retirement. Yet, if it is mainly members of the higher-income groups who receive the lion's share of the benefits from RRSPs, then there is an implicit redistribution of income away from lower-income groups.

Furthermore, to the extent that lower-income earners are less likely to have employer-sponsored pension plans, then the redistribution suggested by Table 3 understates the actual redistribution going on in the Canadian economy.[11]

Benefits to High-Income and Low-Income Contributors

It is misleading to treat all TDSP contributors as if they were identical. The benefits that accrue to low-income and to high-income TDSP contributors differ, and thus TDSPs effect a signifi-

---

11 A lifecycle issue partially confounds the analysis of income distribution here: some of today's noncontributors will be contributors in the future. But there are also large numbers of people who are noncontributors now and will remain such in the future. Thus, it remains true that TDSPs involve a significant redistribution away from noncontributors (of whatever age) to contributors (of whatever age).

Table 3:   *RRSP Contributions by Income Group, 1991*

Income Group	% of Total Contributors	% of Total Contributions	Average Contribution
($)	(%)	(%)	($)
0 – 9,999	9	4	1,310
10,000 – 19,999	15	10	1,700
20,000 – 29,999	21	16	2,060
30,000 – 39,999	20	19	2,540
40,000 – 49,999	15	16	2,970
50,000 – 59,999	9	11	3,510
60,000 – 79,999	7	12	4,660
≥ 80,000	5	12	7,200

Total number of contributors = 4.478 million

Total value of contributors = $12.113 billion

Source: Statistics Canada, *1991 RRSP Room File* (Ottawa, 1993).

cant redistribution of income away from low-income contributors toward higher-income contributors. In doing so, they reverse some of the redistribution that is achieved through income taxes.

The last column of Table 3 shows how the average RRSP contribution varies across income groups.[12] In 1991, the average RRSP contribution for individuals with incomes of less than $10,000 was $1,300; for individuals with incomes of $80,000 or more, it was $7,200.

For analytical purposes, it is helpful to assign RRSP contributors to two income groups. For those contributors with incomes of less than $30,000, the average TDSP contribution in 1991 was $1,803. Given a federal marginal income tax rate of 17 percent, this amount implied a tax rebate in that year of about

---

12 Though Table 3 and the following discussion use data on RRSP contributions only, the basic arguments here apply equally to contributions made to RPPs.

$307. In contrast, for those contributors with incomes of $30,000 or more, the average contribution in 1991 was $3,381; they faced a federal marginal income tax rate of 26 percent, implying a tax rebate of about $879.[13]

The tax rebate in the year of the RRSP contribution does not completely capture the benefits to an individual contributor, so the comparison of $879 to $307 does not completely capture the implicit redistribution of income that occurs as a result of RRSPs. The tax-free accumulation of funds occurring within the RRSP is also important. (The appendix explores this point in more detail.)

Table 4 shows the benefits to hypothetical high- and low-income TDSP contributors who contribute a constant annual amount over 30 years. When both high- and low-income contributors make a contribution equal to $1,803, the average RRSP contribution for low-income individuals (columns 1 and 2), the differences in benefits reflect only the differences in marginal tax rates; high-income contributors benefit more because the TDSP allows them to avoid greater taxation of interest income. When high-income earners make an annual contribution equal to $3,381, the average RRSP contribution for such individuals (column 3), the benefits grow considerably (column 4).[14]

It is clear from Table 4 that the average high-income contributor benefits much more from a TDSP than the average low-income contributor — almost $16,000 more over 30 years. This largess has two sources: high-income contributors are permitted larger TDSP contributions (because the contribution limits are expressed as a percentage of income), and the TDSP successfully avoids taxation at a higher marginal rate. For any

---

13 For simplicity in this example, I ignore the existence of provincial income taxes. Their presence obviously increases marginal tax rates for both income groups, but my basic argument here about the relative benefits of TDSPs to different income groups is still valid. Note also that the stated tax reduction to the upper-income group actually understates the true tax reduction since the highest incomes in this group face a federal marginal rate of 29 percent (rather than the 26 percent assumed in the text).

14 The caveat about lifecycle effects applies here. See footnote 11.

Table 4:   *Benefits^a for High- and Low-Income TDSP Contributors (assuming constant annual contributions)^b*

| | Benefits of Contribution of | | | |
| | $1,803^c$ by | | $3,381^d$ by | |
N^e	Low-Income Earner $(1)^f$	High-Income Earner $(2)^g$	High-Income Earner $(3)^h$	Difference $(3)-(1)$
(years)		*(constant dollars)*		
1	10.18	14.85	27.85	17.67
2	21.10	30.71	57.60	36.50
3	32.80	47.65	89.35	56.55
4	45.34	65.71	123.21	77.87
5	58.75	84.94	159.29	100.54
6	73.08	105.42	197.69	124.61
7	88.38	127.21	238.54	150.16
8	104.71	150.36	281.95	177.24
9	122.11	174.95	328.07	205.96
10	140.65	201.06	377.02	236.37
11	160.38	228.75	428.95	268.57
12	181.37	258.10	484.00	302.63
13	203.69	289.21	542.33	338.64
14	227.39	322.15	604.09	376.70
15	252.56	357.01	669.47	416.91
16	279.28	393.89	738.63	459.35
17	307.61	432.89	811.76	504.15
18	337.64	474.11	889.06	551.42
19	369.47	517.66	970.72	601.25
20	403.17	563.65	1,056.95	653.78
21	438.86	612.19	1,147.98	709.12
22	476.61	663.42	1,244.04	767.43
23	516.56	717.45	1,345.37	828.81
24	558.79	774.42	1,452.21	893.42
25	603.42	834.48	1,564.83	961.41
26	650.58	897.77	1,683.50	1,032.92
27	700.40	964.43	1,808.51	1,108.11
28	752.99	1,034.64	1,940.16	1,187.17
29	808.51	1,108.55	2,078.77	1,270.26
30	867.08	1,186.35	2,224.65	1,357.57
Total	*9,793.46*	*13,633.98*	*25,566.55*	*15,773.09*

Notes to Table 4

[a] See the appendix for details of the calculation of benefits.

[b] Also assuming a constant real interest rate of 4 percent and constant marginal tax rates of 26 percent for high-income contributors and 17 percent for low-income contributors.

[c] The average RRSP contribution for individuals with low income (less than $30,000 per year).

[d] The average RRSP contribution for individuals with high incomes ($30,000 a year or more).

[e] The number of years the contribution accumulates before withdrawal.

[f] $= (\$1,803)\,(0.83)\,[(1.04)^N - (1.0332)^N]$.

[g] $= (\$1,803)\,(0.74)\,[(1.04)^N - (1.0296)^N]$.

[h] $= (\$3,381)\,(0.74)\,[(1.04)^N - (1.0296)^N]$.

value of N, the positive value in the last column of the table illustrates a redistribution of income away from low-income contributors toward high-income contributors.

Summing Up

Given the numbers set out in Tables 3 and 4, it is difficult not to view TDSPs as an effective instrument for achieving a redistribution of income in the *wrong* direction. There is an obvious redistribution of income away from noncontributors toward all TDSP contributors. Moreover, the current system of contribution limits and marginal income tax rates generates a significant redistribution away from low-income contributors toward high-income contributors. When the facts are stated in this way, it is unlikely that the typical Canadian would view TDSPs as a valuable instrument for improving the distribution of income.

That TDSPs are themselves redistributing income in the wrong direction does not necessarily mean that they are an inappropriate part of a tax-and-transfer system that is progressive overall. Indeed, some may argue from a political economy perspective that this "tax gift" to upper-income groups is the payoff necessary to obtain their support of the overall progressivity of the system (with the high top marginal tax rates that such progressivity involves).

One response to such a view is that a simple and transparent tax system has obvious benefits, not the least of which is the honesty it brings to public debate. It would be better to have an up-front policy debate on the appropriate degree of progressivity of the Canadian tax system than to fudge and complicate the issue by having in place several instruments that redistribute income in opposite directions. Moreover, if TDSPs did not exist, there might be less need for high marginal tax rates to reverse the income redistribution that they cause. Thus, eliminating TDSPs may be one way of achieving a desirable flattening of the income tax structure.

A Policy Package

These considerations suggest a package of policies, starting with the abolition of tax-deferred savings plans and going on to address some of the concerns underlying the arguments in favor of TDSPs that I discussed earlier.

Specifically, I propose that the federal government

- abolish all TDSPs;
- reduce income tax rates and raise the GST rate; and
- increase the rate of mandatory saving for retirement.

The debate associated with each proposal could easily fill an entire paper; here, I offer only a brief discussion of how each proposal would achieve or complement the elimination of TDSPs.

It is important that the proposals be viewed as a package, and that the merits of the *entire* package be considered relative to the status quo. In other words, I am not advocating the abolition of TDSPs separately from other policy changes.

Abolish TDSPs

My main policy proposal is to abolish the tax-deferred status of the various retirement savings plans, including RRSPs, firm-sponsored pension plans, and the superannuation plans for the public service. Note that I am not recommending that the plans themselves be abolished — just that their special tax-deferred status be discontinued. For the sake of brevity, however, I speak of the "abolition" or "elimination" of TDSPs.

The abolition of RRSPs would be straightforward. Although individuals obviously could — and would — continue to save for their retirement, contributions to private saving plans would no longer be tax deductible, and income growth within those plans would not be sheltered from taxation.

The abolition of employer-sponsored pension plans would be more complicated, but certainly manageable. RPPs are of two varieties; each must be considered separately, though the same principle of removing the special tax status applies to both. Employer-sponsored pension plans that have "defined contribu-tions," such as money-purchase plans, are effectively RRSPs in which the employer makes contributions in the name of the employee. My proposal is simply to eliminate the tax deductibility of the employee's contributions to such plans and to treat the em-ployer's contributions as current taxable income to the employee.

Employer-sponsored plans of the "defined benefits" variety should also have their special tax status removed. The future benefits to the employee could be converted into an equivalent amount of current income that is taxable along with other current income.[15]

With either type of employer-sponsored pension plan, the elimination of special tax status would ensure that both employ-

---

15 Such a conversion is already done in the computation of the pension adjust-ment (PA) in determining the RRSP room for individuals who have a defined-benefit RPP with their employer. See Horner and Poddar (1992) for details about the PA.

ers and employees view the employers' contributions as ordinary compensation to workers.

Why Not Just Reduce the Generosity of TDSPs? Is there a less drastic way of dealing with the costs imposed by TDSPs? For example, should Canada consider reducing the contribution limits for RRSPs and RPPs or taxing the income generated within the plans? Certainly, this second option has been actively discussed.

The argument against reducing the generosity of TDSPs, rather than abolishing them, is that such a move would not fully address the problem of their redistributing income in the wrong direction. Obviously, a reduction in contribution limits would reduce the possible benefits to TDSP contributors and thus reduce the implicit redistribution of income from noncontributors toward contributors, but the basic system would still be providing "upside-down" assistance (Ingerman and Rowley 1994). Unless policy has the direct and stated goal of redistributing income away from the poor toward the rich, TDSPs should not exist at all.

The argument against trying to reduce the benefits of TDSPs by levying a tax on the income earned within the plans is based on administrative ease. Despite the problems that exist with TDSPs, it can be said that the Canadian system is at least coherent: the tax deductibility of contributions and the tax avoidance of capital income go hand-in-hand. To permit the up-front tax deductibility of contributions while levying a tax on the capital income earned with the plan would generate a considerable administrative burden. For example, would withdrawals from a plan be added to taxable income, or would only some fraction of them be considered taxable?

Reduce Income Tax Rates and Raise the GST

Given a desire to avoid the distortionary effects on the return to saving caused by the taxation of capital income, the desire for reforming the Canadian tax system — as reflected in the 1987 income tax reforms and the 1991 introduction of the GST — is certainly appropriate. In general terms, such reform aims to reduce the emphasis on income taxes and increase the emphasis on consumption taxes.

This process of tax reform could proceed in two alternative ways. First, the current income tax system could be modified so as to tax wage income but exempt capital income. Unfortunately, although taking this course would remove the distortion to the rate of return to saving,[16] it would introduce other distortions; since different types of income are taxed at different rates, it would reduce the horizontal equity in the tax system.

An easier way to proceed toward a consumption-based tax system is to reduce income tax rates across the board and simultaneously increase the rate on the GST. Given that both tax systems are already in place, such a change would be administratively easy. It would also be successful in reducing the distortion caused by interest taxation. At the same time, the tax base for the GST should be widened by removing all exemptions. The considerable administrative advantages of an exemption-free GST make this option more attractive than simply exempting interest income within an income tax system.

Since the elimination of TDSPs would end a considerable amount of inappropriate income redistribution, there would be less pressure on the tax-and-transfer system to undo this redistribution by transferring resources from high-income to low-income people — that is, there would be less pressure on the tax system to be progressive. Thus, when income tax rates were lowered across the board (and the GST raised), the entire structure could also be flattened. The importance of this possibility should not be overlooked. As Dahlby (1994) clearly demonstrates, the current

---

16 Since capital income is the return on saving, a tax on wage income alone is equivalent to a consumption tax in the sense that neither system distorts the return to saving (Atkinson and Stiglitz 1980).

combination of federal and provincial taxes and transfers makes the schedule of marginal income tax rates look more like a mountain range than a plateau. To the extent that policymakers care about the effects of distortionary taxation, these mountain ranges should be a real source of concern.

Why Not Eliminate Income Taxes Altogether? If a move toward increased consumption taxation is desirable, does it not it follow that the complete elimination of income taxes would be even better? The short answer is, almost certainly no. To the extent that the government is still committed to the principle of income redistribution, the obvious way to identify and reach people in need of assistance is through the income tax system. The complete elimination of income taxes would greatly complicate the process of identifying these people and redistributing resources in their direction. One advantage of increasing the GST rate but keeping the basic income tax structure in place (albeit with lower rates) is that the income tax system could still be used as a means of identifying and assisting low-income earners.

Increase the Role of Mandatory Saving

Given the proposed abolition of TDSPs, is there anything government could do to encourage individuals to save more for their retirement so that the pressures on the public purse would be reduced? Canadian governments cannot credibly commit themselves to denying income support to individuals who have failed to take the opportunity to save for their own retirement. But they could solve the saving-incentive problem and reduce future demands on the public purse by increasing the role of mandatory saving.

Of course, Canada has an established system of mandatory saving. Most individuals are now required to save through the

CPP/QPP. These programs have recently come under public scrutiny as it has become clear that their pay-as-you-go nature is leading to considerable problems concerning their sustainability.[17]

Yet mandatory saving need not be exclusively identified with these public pension systems. One could reasonably argue that, by promoting an increased role for mandatory saving not necessarily in the guise of the current CPP/QPP programs, I am simply suggesting a reform of the public pension system. But it would be a significant reform. Particularly desirable in my view would be two changes: an increase in mandatory contributions and a move to professional private management of the public pension funds.

Increase Mandatory Contributions. Mandatory contributions should be raised to a level that can be expected to finance a moderate level of retirement consumption, given an average number of working years. This increase would force individuals to save more for their retirement than they are doing through the current public pension plans. Once this change worked its way through the age structure of the population, the need for the government to provide income support for retired people would be reduced. The government would still assist low-income individuals (of whatever age), but the problem of individuals' not saving enough for their own retirement could be largely eliminated.

Private Management of Mandatory Saving. In the current public pension system, the unfunded nature of the programs has encountered several problems, including changing demographics and the actions of cash-strapped governments. Individuals correctly view their contributions to an unfunded public pension system as an investment with a very uncertain rate of return. But

---

17 For a discussion of some current problems with the CPP, see Robson (1996) and Robson's paper in this volume.

the uncertainty is not the usual worries about the real interest rate; instead, it is focused on the rate of population growth and the nature of demographic shifts in the population. To make matters worse, as long as the public pension system remains within reach of financially strapped governments, there is perpetual fear that profligate government spending will deplete the pool of pension funds and thus necessitate increases in the contribution rates.

There is no practical way to eliminate the fundamental rate-of-return uncertainty faced by individual savers, but it is easy in principle to avoid the problems of demographics and financially strapped governments. Though individuals may be legally required to make regular contributions to the public saving plans, there is no reason the management of these funds could not be entirely beyond the reach of government. They could be invested in private mutual funds and managed professionally. Individuals could simply be required to make deposits with any one (or more) of a number of accredited fund managers.

The pension system I have just described — mandatory contributions and private management of funds — is essentially the system that has been adopted in the past decade in Chile and imitated by other South American countries. Though this type of system is not without its own problems, many analysts think it has considerable merit (see Diamond 1996; and Diamond and Valdes-Prieto 1994 for details).

A Crucial Caveat

The current federal minister of finance, Paul Martin, has steered his way through three years of managing Canada's public finances with considerable deftness. In the 1995 and 1996 budgets, he outlined his plans for the reduction of the federal budget deficit, and he is on target for reducing the deficit to 3 percent of gross domestic product by 1997. With the Canadian economy showing solid performance in terms of real economic growth and continued low inflation (despite the reluctance of the unemployment rate to fall below about 9.5 percent), it seems clear that keeping deficit reduction on track will remain near the top of Martin's list of goals for the foreseeable future. Throughout 1994 and 1995, the possibilities of reducing the generosity of RRSPs and RPPs received considerable attention. In some cases, the talk was about reducing the contribution limits; in others, the suggestions involved levying a tax on income earned within the plans. In both cases, the motivation was clear: to reduce the generosity of RRSPs and RPPs as a means of reducing the budget deficit.

Nevertheless, the case against TDSPs would have as much merit in a world of a $25 billion surplus as in a world of a $25 billion deficit. None of the arguments I have leveled against TDSPs relies on the existence of a government fiscal deficit. The effects of TDSPs on the distribution of income are largely independent of the government's fiscal position. Even my discussion of the effect of TDSPs on government income tax revenue applies equally well to any overall fiscal position of the government. Whether the government is currently saving a lot or only a little (or borrowing a lot or only a little), the existence of TDSPs will reduce its saving below the level that would otherwise exist.

I emphasize, therefore, that none of the arguments presented here for abolishing TDSPs is motivated in any way by concern over the current government's need to substantially reduce the fiscal deficit. Indeed, I believe it would be a mistake to eliminate TDSPs as a deficit-cutting measure. Their abolition would represent a significant increase in the overall taxation of households. Though the elimination of tax-assisted saving — a tax increase by any other name — would not be felt equally by all Canadians, it would still represent a significant increase in taxes overall.

Conceptually separating the idea of eliminating TDSPs from the issues surrounding deficit reduction has a clear and important implication for the proposals outlined in the previous section. The combination of my first two main policy proposals — abolishing TDSPs plus lowering income tax rates and raising the GST — should be approximately revenue neutral.[18]

Closing Remarks

I have argued that all TDSPs should be abolished. None of the three main arguments supporting them provides a strong defense of such plans. First, it seems doubtful that TDSPs increase national saving (even if such an increase were a sensible goal, a matter that is justifiably controversial). Second, although few people question the desirability of reducing the need for government-financed retirement income support, the voluntary nature of TDSPs makes them a poor solution to the saving-incentive problem; mandatory saving through higher contributions to a modified public pension plan would be more effective. Finally, if one overall goal of tax reform is to move away from income taxation toward consumption taxation, there are easier routes than TDSPs; a straightforward reduction in income tax rates and increase in the GST would be more effective.

TDSPs are the last great tax loophole for middle- and upper-income Canadians. But it is noncontributors (who tend to have low incomes) and low-income contributors who are footing the bill for these benefits. The irony, of course, is that, while low-income individuals are being hurt by the existence of TDSPs, they are probably among the strong supporters of a policy that allows such tax-deferred saving. The reason is simple: most individuals are not cognizant of the overall effects of TDSPs on government tax revenues and certainly do not recognize the implicit income redistributions that are occurring.

Although TDSPs impose significant costs and produce little in the way of benefits, it is important that policymakers give

---

18 The mandatory private pension contributions should be viewed as neither a tax on individuals nor a source of tax revenue since these items ideally would be kept completely off the government's books.

considerable thought to devising the least costly manner of their elimination. In particular, the treatment of funds inside existing TDSPs would demand careful attention. I have not discussed such transition issues here, but they must be addressed if my main proposal is to be considered at all seriously.

One possibility is to prohibit both the creation of new TDSPs and the expansion of existing ones, but to allow those that exist to mature according to the current rules. A preferable (though slightly more drastic) alternative is to require all funds within existing TDSPs to be transferred immediately into registered retirement income funds (RRIFs). Withdrawals from such funds, which are classified as taxable income, could then take place according to the existing rules over a period of, say, ten years.

Abolishing TDSPs altogether would clearly be an extreme policy decision, and it may be natural to think that their elimination would leave a void in the existing tax-and-transfer system. For this reason, I have also presented a package of complementary policy proposals. Perhaps the most important one is a move toward a Chilean-style system of mandatory individual pension contributions that are managed privately by professional fund managers. Such mandatory private saving would allow the government to reduce expenditures on income-support programs yet have no direct negative effect on the level of income tax revenue.

Finally, I have emphasized that the abolition of TDSPs should not be motivated by a desire to reduce the federal government's fiscal deficit. Though that abolition would certainly lead to a significant increase in tax revenue for both provincial and federal governments, it is a reduction in government expenditure that seems to me a more appropriate solution to the current fiscal situation. Thus, my proposals to abolish TDSPs, reduce income tax rates, and increase (and broaden) the GST should be designed as a revenue-neutral policy package.

Appendix: The Benefits of Contributing to TDSPs

The size of a taxpayer's contribution, his marginal tax rate, and the number of years of accumulation all combine to generate the benefits from contributing to a TDSP relative to saving outside a TDSP. The illustrations below use the following notation: N is the number of years an individual contribution is allowed to accumulate before withdrawal, r is the annual real interest rate, and τ is the individual's marginal income tax rate.

An individual who saves X dollars today *outside* a TDSP will receive

$$R_1 = X \left[1 + r(1 - \tau)\right]^N \tag{1}$$

after-tax dollars in N years.

In contrast, consider an individual who faces the same tax rate but contributes X dollars to a TDSP today and saves the tax rebate outside of the TDSP. (Requiring this person to save the tax rebate from the TDSP ensures that the two hypothetical individuals have the same level of current consumption. Thus, the difference in after-tax dollars N years in the future captures the full benefit of the TDSP.)

The latter individual will receive

$$R_2 = X (1 + r)^N (1 - \tau) + (\tau X) \left[1 + r(1 - \tau)\right]^N \tag{2}$$

after-tax dollars in N years. The first term in Equation (2) represents the after-tax withdrawal of the principal and interest from the TDSP; the second term is the accumulation on the initial tax refund, τX, that the individual receives as a result of making the TDSP contribution.

The benefit to an individual from contributing to a TDSP in any given year, relative to saving that same amount outside the TDSP, is therefore equal to

$$R_2 - R_1 = X (1 - \tau) \left\{ (1 + r)^N - \left[1 + r(1 - \tau)\right]^N \right\}, \tag{3}$$

which is positive as long as the individual faces a positive (and less than 100 percent) marginal income tax rate. The direct benefit of TDSPs to the contributor comes from the fact that such plans permit contributions to accumulate tax free (which makes the expression in braces greater than zero). Given the presence of this tax-free accumulation, the larger is the initial TDSP contribution, the greater the benefit.[19]

Equation (3) shows clearly the relative benefits to high- and low-income TDSP contributors and also reveals the size of the implicit income redistribution generated by TDSPs. To keep things simple, suppose there are two types of contributors, high income and low income, both of whom make a single contribution to a TDSP to be withdrawn N years in the future. Using the average RRSP contributions (calculated from Table 3), a real interest rate of 4 percent, and a value of N equal to 30 years, one can calculate the benefits for the two types of contributors as:

high-income benefit =

$$(\$3,381)\,(1 - 0.26)\,\{(1.04)^{30} - [1 + (0.04)(1 - 0.26)]^{30}\} = \$2,224.65\;;$$

low-income benefit =

$$(\$1,803)\,(1 - 0.17)\,\{(1.04)^{30} - [1 + (0.04)(1 - 0.17)]^{30}\} = \$867.08\;.$$

Note that these benefits are expressed in terms of real dollars 30 years in the future: their present value would be considerably smaller. But it is the *relative* benefits to the two types of contributors that are of interest, and they can be viewed in either present or future dollars. Note also that these are the benefits that accrue to the two individuals from only *one* year's worth of TDSP contributions. The relative benefits over 30 years are shown in Table 4.

---

19 Another benefit arises if withdrawals are made when the individual is in a tax bracket lower than his bracket when he made the contributions. But the flattening of the tax system following the 1987 income tax reform suggests that, for many people, this effect will be either absent or quite small.

References

Atkinson, A., and J. Stiglitz. 1980. *Lectures on Public Economics*. New York: McGraw Hill.

Canada. Various years. Department of National Revenue. *Taxation Statistics*. Annual. Ottawa: Supply and Services Canada.

———. 1994. Department of Finance. *Government of Canada Tax Expenditures*. December.

Dahlby, B. 1994. "The Distortionary Effect of Rising Taxes." In W. Robson and W. Scarth, eds., *Deficit Reduction: What Pain, What Gain?* Policy Study 23. Toronto: C.D. Howe Institute.

Diamond, P. 1996. "Public Provision of Pensions: The Doug Purvis Memorial Lecture." *Canadian Public Policy* 22 (March): 1–6.

———, and S. Valdes-Prieto. 1994. "Social Security Reform." In B. Bosworth, R. Dornbusch, and R. Laban, eds., *The Chilean Economy*. Washington, DC: Brookings Institution.

Gale, W., and J. Scholz. 1994. "IRAs and Household Saving." *American Economic Review* 84 (December): 1233–1260.

Horner, K., and S. Poddar. 1992. "Pension Reform in Canada." International Institute of Public Finance. Mimeographed.

Ingerman, S., and R. Rowley. 1994. "Tax Expenditures and Retirement Savings." *Canadian Business Economics*, Summer, pp. 46–55.

Ragan, C. 1994. "Progressive Income Taxes and the Substitution Effect of RRSPs." *Canadian Journal of Economics* 27 (February): 43–57.

Robson, W.B.P. 1996. *Putting Some Gold in the Golden Years: Fixing the Canada Pension Plan*. C.D. Howe Institute Commentary 76. Toronto: C.D. Howe Institute, January.

Venti, S., and D. Wise. 1990. "Have IRAs Increased US Saving?" *Quarterly Journal of Economics* 105 (August): 661–698.

———, and D. Wise. 1994. "RRSPs and Saving in Canada." Mimeographed.

Public Pensions in Canada

John B. Burbidge

Intergenerational transfers occur within every society. Those who are able to provide for more than their own needs directly or indirectly provide resources to those who are imperfectly able to care for themselves. In Canada today, for example, taxes levied on prime-age workers are used to cover the costs of educating the young and public pensions for the elderly. While the form and extent of these transfers no doubt vary enormously across different societies and within any society over time, each society must somehow choose from the set of all possible transfers a particular allocation that is, for whatever reasons, most appealing.

Analysis of public pensions is facilitated by distinguishing the collection of all transfers that might be made from the particular one chosen. The former — the collection of feasible transfers — depends on many factors, including the age distribution of the population and the society's ability to produce goods and services. The latter must strike some sort of balance between the interests of those who are taxed (for example, prime-age workers) and those who benefit (for example, the young through the educational system, or the old through public pensions); that is, it must embody the society's notion of intergenerational equity. Different people looking at the same set of facts about which transfers to make may have widely disparate opinions on inter-

The first draft of this paper was written while I held the Faculty of Social Science Chair in Public Policy at the University of Western Ontario. I am most grateful to this institution for its hospitality and financial support. In addition, I thank John Richards, Bill Robson, and Bill Watson for very helpful comments.

generational equity — that is, which of the feasible transfers should be made.

Most of this paper presents facts about public pensions in Canada to inform the discussion of which changes, if any, one might wish to pursue. I also suggest two possible reforms I plan to explore in subsequent research. These suggested reforms reflect my judgment on intergenerational equity, which may well differ sharply from that of many, or even most, readers.

High rates of economic growth during the 1950s and 1960s and the declining ratio of elderly people to young people associated with the baby boom greatly expanded feasible intergenerational transfers to the elderly in many developed economies. It is hardly surprising that these two decades witnessed the introduction and expansion of many public pension programs in Canada, the United States, and elsewhere, but slower rates of growth since 1973 have diminished feasible transfers. At first, governments borrowed domestically and internationally in order to postpone having to cut intergenerational transfers, but persistently lower rates of productivity growth eventually forced successor governments to deal with their debt problem, in some cases by implementing cuts in intergenerational transfers that were much larger than would have occurred had earlier governments been more responsible.

One theme of this paper is that stagnant or falling real earnings of prime-age workers since the mid-1970s imply that the set of intergenerational transfers feasible in the long term today is smaller than it was 20 years ago. If society's views on intergenerational equity have not changed, reductions in transfers to the elderly are probably in order. A second theme is that no particular collection of public pension programs is appropriate for long periods; the extent of public assistance for the elderly should be tied more closely to the well-being of those whose taxes cover the cost of public pensions.

This paper begins with a review of the major components of the public pension system in Canada, followed by an examination of the economic literature and some empirical evidence that suggests that the efficiency losses caused by balanced-budget expansions in public pensions have been exaggerated. This leads into the final section, which presents evidence to support the view that an imbalance in intergenerational equity has emerged over the past 20 years.

Current Programs

The many documents on reforming public pensions in Canada conceive of the retirement income system working through three distinct channels:

- the federal and provincial public pension programs such as Old Age Security (OAS), the Guaranteed Income Supplement (GIS), the Canada and Quebec Pension Plans (CPP/QPP), and Ontario's Guaranteed Annual Income Supplement (GAINS);
- work-related private pension plans, which are regulated federally by the *Pension Benefits Standards Act* and provincially by similar acts; and
- the federal *Income Tax Act*, which provides incentives for private saving, such as Registered Retirement Savings Plans (RRSPs).

This paper focuses on the first, but policymakers contemplating changes in Canada's retirement income system must deal with all three simultaneously.

Pension reform documents argue that the primary purpose of public programs such as OAS and the GIS is to create a social safety net for the incomes of elderly Canadians and that the CPP/QPP, in conjunction with private pensions and other tax-assisted savings vehicles, serve to maintain relative standards of living upon retirement or disability.

In fiscal year 1993/94, the OAS budget was estimated at $15.4 billion, the GIS budget at $4.3 billion, and the CPP at

$14.5 billion in benefit payments (and another $3 billion for the QPP).[1] Several provinces and territories also provide additional means-tested payments to the elderly, and many provinces and municipalities provide transfers in the form of subsidized services (medicare, homes for the aged, and so on).

OAS, the GIS, and the Spousal Pension Allowance

OAS is payable to anyone 65 years of age or older who meets certain residency requirements. One way for an individual to meet this requirement is to have lived in Canada for ten years immediately preceding the date on which his or her application is approved. As of April 1, 1994, the maximum pension was $387.74 per month, or $4,653 per annum. It has been indexed, quarterly, to the consumer price index (CPI) since April 1, 1973, but an amendment passed in February 1983 placed a cap on the indexing factor of 1.5 percent per quarter (6 percent per annum) for the last three quarters of 1983 and 1.25 percent per quarter (5 percent per annum) for 1984. Table 1 shows the value of OAS payments for selected years from its inception in 1952 until April 1993. During the postwar boom years (1952–67), they rose by nearly 60 percent, then fell somewhat during the inflation of the early 1970s, and have been remarkably constant since 1975.

OAS is taxable under the *Income Tax Act*, and the social benefits repayment tax (line 235 of the income tax form) claws back OAS from higher-income individuals. For example, in 1993, OAS for a single individual was reduced by 15 cents per dollar of net income exceeding $53,215, until net OAS equaled zero at a net income of $84,234. For lower-income households, the taxes that would otherwise be paid on OAS benefits are largely offset by the nonrefundable age tax credit which is available to everyone 65 years and over, and which stood at $3,482 in 1993.

---

1 The federal Liberals, not the federal Progressive Conservatives, were the first (in 1983) to cap these pensions. The decrease in the inflation rate after 1982 meant the cap had only a minor effect on these pensions.

Table 1: *Maximum Monthly Pensions under the Old Age Security Act, Selected Years 1952–93*

Date Effective	Basic OAS	Guaranteed Income Supplement		Maximum Pension	
		Individual	Married Couple	Individual	Married Couple
		(April 1993 dollars)			
Jan. 1, 1952	237			237	
Jan. 1, 1967	361	144		505	
Apr. 1, 1971	329	226	391	555	1,048
Jan. 1, 1975	370	259	460	629	1,200
Jan. 1, 1980	371	305	507	676	1,250
Jan. 1, 1983	378	380	586	758	1,343
Jan. 1, 1984	377	380	586	757	1,341
Jan. 1, 1985	378	449	585	827	1,341
Jan. 1, 1986	377	448	583	825	1,337
Jan. 1, 1987	378	450	586	828	1,342
Jan. 1, 1988	380	451	588	831	1,347
Jan. 1, 1989	379	450	586	829	1,343
Jan. 1, 1990	378	449	585	826	1,340
Jan. 1, 1991	369	438	571	807	1,309
Jan. 1, 1992	383	455	592	837	1,358
Apr. 1, 1992	381	453	590	834	1,353
July 1, 1992	381	452	589	833	1,351
Oct. 1, 1992	382	454	592	837	1,356
Jan. 1, 1993	380	451	588	831	1,348
Apr. 1, 1993	382	453	591	835	1,354

Note: Data were converted to April 1993 dollars using the all-items consumer price index.
Source: CTF 1993, table 9.1.

The GIS is an income-tested supplement payable to OAS recipients. Introduced in 1967 as a "temporary" program to help low-income elderly through the ten-year phase-in period of the CPP, the GIS has become a key component of the social safety net for elderly Canadians. As of April 1, 1994, the maximum GIS was $460.79 per month for a single pensioner and $300.14 for each member of a married couple, both of whom had to be at least 65 years of age. The "recapture rate" or "taxback rate" for the GIS is 50 percent on any non-OAS/GIS income.[2] If one member of the couple is ineligible for both OAS and the spousal pension allowance (SPA), the rules for the GIS are slightly different — the benefits are the same as those for a single pensioner, except that the first $4,700 of income over and above OAS and the GIS is ignored, and the taxback rate is only 25 percent on the couple's combined yearly income.

GIS benefits have been indexed to the CPI since 1972. Table 1 shows that the maximum GIS for a single individual rose briskly from $144 per month in 1967 to $380 per month in 1983, then jumped by nearly 20 percent to $450 per month in 1985, and has been very stable at that level ever since. GIS benefits for married couples also rose sharply between 1971 and 1983, and have been constant at around $590 per month since then. by combining OAS and the GIS, one may deduce from Table 1 that, over the past decade, the federal government has guaranteed an income of $10,000 (in 1993 dollars) per annum to elderly individuals and $16,200 to elderly married couples.

In 1975, the *Old Age Security Act* was amended to provide an income-tested pension, the spousal pension allowance, to 60-to-64-year-old spouses of OAS recipients. In effect, the SPA guarantees the same minimum level of income to a couple in which one person is aged 60 to 64 as to a couple where both are over 65. The maximum SPA is thus $687.88 (387.74 plus 300.14) per month, as of April 1, 1994. The taxback rates are 75 percent

---

2 This means that, for each extra dollar of income, GIS payments decrease by 50 cents.

of family income until the OAS component of the SPA is exhausted, then 50 percent of total family income until each spouse's GIS payment is equal to $127.50 per month, at which point the rate drops to 25 percent until the rest of the SPA is exhausted.[3] To eliminate the SPA completely, the couple would have to receive about $20,610 per annum in outside income. If an OAS recipient dies, leaving a spouse aged 60 to 64, the survivor may be eligible for a "widowed" spousal allowance. As of April 1, 1994, the maximum benefit is $759.42 per month, with a taxback rate of 75 percent on yearly outside income until the first half of this pension is eliminated, at which point the taxback rate drops to 50 percent. The SPA is thus available to all those aged 60 to 64 who are not single, separated, or divorced.

The number of recipients and annual payments for OAS, the GIS, and the SPA are shown in Table 2. While the number of OAS recipients has grown by more than one-quarter over the past decade, the number of GIS recipients peaked in 1989 and the number of SPA recipients peaked a year earlier. The rising total of OAS payments reflects the growing number of elderly people, since almost everyone over age 65 gets OAS. Overall outlays for the income-tested programs, the GIS and the SPA, have been falling in real terms since the mid-1980s, despite a virtually constant GIS level in real terms (see Table 1), which suggests that real incomes of the elderly have been rising, a point to which I return below.

Finally, there is a great variety of provincial and territorial supplements to these federal programs. However, all stipulate a fairly strict residency requirement and almost all have quite high taxback rates, which, in conjunction with those for the GIS and the SPA, imply marginal tax rates of 100 percent or greater on outside income. For example, Ontario operates a program called the Guaranteed Annual Income Supplement, which pays a maxi-

---

[3] Note that $12 \times 387.74/0.75 + 2 ([300.14 - 127.50]/0.5) + 127.50/0.25$ equals $20,610.56, which in turn equals $12 \times 387.74/0.75 + 2(300.14/0.5)$.

Table 2: *Old Age Security Recipients and Payments, fiscal years 1983/84 to 1993/94*

	Recipients (March)			Payments			
	OAS	GIS	SPA	OAS	GIS	SPA	Total
	(number)			(1993 $ millions)			
1983/84	2,490,881	1,246,119	87,890	11,125	3,672	339	15,135
1984/85	2,569,448	1,296,545	93,114	11,552	4,152	350	16,053
1985/86	2,652,234	1,329,886	142,302	11,953	4,479	469	16,902
1986/87	2,748,504	1,345,391	125,188	12,314	4,464	612	17,390
1987/88	2,835,107	1,356,672	140,159	12,703	4,485	598	17,786
1988/89	2,919,398	1,363,532	134,279	13,046	4,481	563	18,091
1989/90	3,005,803	1,359,096	127,308	13,371	4,382	523	18,276
1990/91	3,098,506	1,346,483	120,929	13,804	4,243	455	18,502
1991/92 (est.)	3,180,498	1,329,090	115,805	14,289	4,283	461	19,033
1992/93	n.a.	n.a.	n.a.	15,071	4,324	474	19,869
1993/94 (est.)	n.a.	n.a.	n.a.	15,424	4,331	444	20,199

Note: Payments data were converted to October 1993 dollars using the all-items consumer price index.
Source: CTF 1993, table 9.2.

mum of about $80 per month to Ontario residents who were in receipt of the GIS (recipients of the SPA are excluded). As of April 1, 1994, this has brought the guaranteed income of an individual to $927.31 per month and that of a married couple to $1,534.92 per month. Since the taxback rate for both the GAINS and the GIS is 50 percent on non-OAS/GIS/ GAINS income, these rules imply that GAINS recipients face a tax rate of 100 percent on outside income. This is a extraordinarily strong inducement to retire from the labor market, a point I expand on in the section entitled "Effects of Current Programs."

The Canada Pension Plan

The CPP became law in 1965, contributions began on January 1, 1966, and benefits were first paid on January 1, 1967. The CPP is a compulsory, contributory pension plan which pays benefits in a variety of circumstances and which requires those working to make certain contributions.

Retirement pensions are based on what may be termed the individual's earnings history since January 1, 1966, or since attaining age 18, whichever occurs more recently. For each year, a calculation is made of the ratio of earnings to yearly maximum pensionable earnings (YMPE), which becomes an element of the individual's earnings history (the upper bound on all elements in the earnings history is unity).[4] The retirement pension available at age 65 follows the formula:

CPP benefit = 0.25 × (average ratio of annual earnings to YMPE over lifetime earnings) × (average YMPE for last three years of work, including the year of retirement).

For example, someone who had always earned at least YMPE and who retired in 1993 would receive $667.36 per month (equal to

---

4 In making these calculations, the federal government drops the lowest 15 percent of numbers from the earnings history and the numbers for any years spent caring for children under the age of seven.

one-quarter of the average YMPE over the years 1991–93). These numbers are shown in Table 3, which also contains data on YMPE for selected years since 1966.

So far, the discussion has assumed retirement at age 65, but the CPP admits the possibility of starting a retirement pension any time between ages 60 and 70. In that case, the pension is reduced by 0.5 percent for each month under age 65 and increased by 0.5 percent for each month over age 65. For example, in 1993, a 60-year-old (who had always earned at least YMPE) could have chosen to retire and collect CPP benefits of $467.15 per month — that is, 70 percent of $667.36. Once a person's initial benefits have been determined, they are indexed annually to the October-over-October change in the CPI. Table 3 shows that the real value of retirement pensions rose rapidly through the ten-year phase-in period of the CPP, continued to rise until 1988, fell slowly from 1988 until 1991, and have risen slowly since 1991. When the CPP was created in 1966, it was intended that YMPE eventually would equal the average industrial wage as measured by Statistics Canada and, indeed, during the 1980s, the growth rate of YMPE was increased to 12.5 percent per annum, reaching the average industrial wage by 1986.

The orphan's benefit is a benefit, reduced by 50 percent for each of more than four orphans per family, payable to the children of a deceased contributor who are under 18 years of age or between the ages of 18 and 25 and in full-time attendance at school. From 1967 until 1992, this benefit hovered near $120 per month (in 1993 dollars); it was then raised significantly, and stood at $157.48 per month as of January 1, 1993 (see Table 3).

The spouse's benefit is payable to a deceased contributor's spouse who is over 45, disabled, or has dependent children.[5] Until 1992, the formula was a lump sum equal to the orphan's benefit plus three-eighths of the retirement pension to which the deceased was entitled. Since 1992, the growth rates in both spouse's and disabled benefits have matched the lower of the growth rate

---

5 This is payable whether or not the person is working or remarries.

in YMPE and retirement benefits. Slightly reduced pensions are payable to spouses between ages 34 and 45 who are not disabled and who do not have dependent children. Again, once this pension has been determined, it is indexed to the CPI; on attaining age 65, this person would receive 60 percent of the deceased's pension.

Disability pensions are paid to contributors who are no longer able to work. Until 1987, they equaled the orphan's benefit plus three-quarters of the retirement pension to which the individual was entitled. On April 1, 1987, this pension was increased by $150 per month. On turning 65, the disabled person now receives a full retirement pension, with the years during which the person has been unable to work dropped from the earnings history. The CPP also provides a death benefit equal to the smaller of 10 percent of YMPE or 6 times the deceased's monthly retirement pension.

The CPP programs are financed by a proportional tax on earnings between the exemption level (see Table 3) and YMPE. In 1993, employers and employees each paid 2.5 percent, while the self-employed contributed 5 percent. To get agreement with the provinces when the CPP was introduced in 1965, the federal government set the contribution rate so that revenues would exceed expenditures, and the provinces were permitted to borrow from the resultant fund at below-market interest rates. As Table 4 shows, it is only very recently that expenditures have exceeded revenues. As the number of recipients has grown, payroll taxes have increased, but not by enough to keep increasing the stock of assets held by the CPP (currently about $40 billion). The table clearly shows that the CPP has become a "pay-as-you-go" system (like the social security program in place in the United States) whereby each year's taxes are sufficient only to meet each year's expenditures.[6] I shall return to this subject below.

---

6 The CPP could run down its assets by calling in loans from the provinces, but I suspect this would only cause yet another federal-provincial row. Even so, the assets would cover only about three years of expenditures. Viewing the CPP in private pension terms, it is clear that CPP has a large unfunded liability.

Table 3: *Canada Pension Plan Monthly Contributions and Benefits, Selected Years 1966–93*

Date Effective	Exempt Earnings	Yearly Maximum Pensionable Earnings	Maximum Contributions[a]	Retirement	Surviving Spouse under Age 65	Orphan	Disability
				(current dollars)			
Jan. 1, 1966	600	5,000	79.20				
Jan. 1, 1970	600	5,300	84.60	43.33	67.16	26.53	92.88[b]
Jan. 1, 1975	700	7,400	120.60	122.50	88.31	37.27	139.35
Jan. 1, 1980	1,300	13,100	212.40	244.44	148.92	57.25	240.58
Jan. 1, 1985	2,300	23,400	379.80	435.42	250.84	87.56	414.13
Jan. 1, 1988	2,600	26,500	478.00	543.06	302.61	98.96	660.94
Jan. 1, 1989	2,700	27,700	525.00	556.25	315.02	103.02	681.25
Jan. 1, 1990	2,800	28,900	574.20	577.08	324.37	107.96	709.52
Jan. 1, 1991	3,000	30,500	632.50	604.86	339.96	113.14	743.64
Jan. 1, 1992	3,200	32,200	696.00	636.11	358.24	154.70	783.89
Jan. 1, 1993	3,300	33,400	752.50	667.36	372.11	157.48	812.85

(January 1993 dollars)[c]

Jan. 1, 1966	2,979	24,828	393.27			
Jan. 1, 1970	2,533	22,374	357.14	182.92	283.52	112.00	392.09
Jan. 1, 1975	2,150	22,726	370.37	376.21	271.21	114.46	427.96
Jan. 1, 1980	2,641	26,611	431.46	496.54	302.51	116.29	488.70
Jan. 1, 1985	3,168	32,228	523.08	599.69	345.47	120.59	570.36
Jan. 1, 1988	3,170	32,309	582.77	662.09	368.94	120.65	805.81
Jan. 1, 1989	3,155	32,371	613.53	650.05	368.14	120.39	796.12
Jan. 1, 1990	3,102	32,012	636.04	639.23	359.30	119.59	785.93
Jan. 1, 1991	3,110	31,622	655.78	627.12	352.47	117.30	771.01
Jan. 1, 1992	3,266	32,859	710.25	649.13	365.57	157.87	799.94
Jan. 1, 1993	3,300	33,400	752.50	667.36	372.11	157.48	812.85

[a] Employers and employees *each* pay these amounts; self-employed individuals pay twice these amounts.
[b] Effective February 1970.
[c] Data were converted to January 1993 dollars using the all-items consumer price index.
Source: CTF 1993, table 9.

Table 4: Canada Pension Plan Recipients, Revenues, and Expenditures, Selected fiscal years 1966/67 to 1993/94

	Number of Recipients[a]	Total Contri- butions	Other	Total	Benefit Payments	Admini- strative Expenses	Net Increase in Account	Funds Transferred to CPP Invest- ment Fund
						(January 1994 $ millions except as noted)[b]		
1966/67	3,475	2,856	62	2,917	0	41	2,876	2,824
1969/70	160,070	3,189	615	3,805	202	76	3,526	3,463
1974/75	631,726	3,854	1,614	5,468	1,241	93	4,134	3,998
1978/80	1,213,998	4,872	2,653	7,525	3,365	120	4,040	3,845
1984/85	1,723,444	5,413	4,030	9,443	5,893	140	3,411	3,138
1987/88	2,289,550	6,896	4,532	11,429	9,053	167	2,209	2,646
1988/89	2,523,121	7,398	4,632	12,030	9,998	158	1,873	2,444
1989/90	2,674,194	8,168	4,693	12,861	10,631	163	2,068	2,517
1990/91	2,819,145	8,370	4,633	13,004	11,073	171	1,759	2,146
1991/92	2,972,171	8,675	4,614	13,289	12,192	139	958	2,155
1992/93 (est.)	n.a.	9,650	4,495	14,145	13,523	175	447	924
1993/94 (est.)	n.a.	10,000	4,506	14,506	14,468	174	− 136	

[a] As of March 31.
[b] Data were converted to January 1994 dollars using the all-items consumer price index.
Source: CTF 1993, table 9.11.

It is important to realize from this brief description of the current Canadian public pension system that, however accustomed to it we may be, it is quite new. Only a few decades ago, Canada had a completely different system of support for the elderly, one dominated by private arrangements such as those that existed within the nineteenth-century family.[7] Taking a quick look back at how that system operated will help to highlight some of the problems in the current system.

The nineteenth-century family system was forced to confront changing economic circumstances immediately. Families were unable to borrow large sums of money, so a poor crop on the farm or the loss of work in the city meant that everyone in the multigenerational household ate less. Compare this with the slowness with which modern governments adjusted to the reality of reduced economic growth after 1973 — witness, for example, the difficulties the Mulroney government faced in attempting to de-index OAS in 1985. Over the past two decades, successive Canadian governments have tax- and debt-financed transfers to the elderly, but Canadians' generous instincts with respect to the elderly and to the recipients of other public programs have left the country with a debt problem. Its citizens have repeatedly told all levels of government that they will not tolerate higher taxes. Obviously, there is much more inertia in the current public system than there was in the former private system.

On the other hand, the current system provides better insurance across and within generations than did the earlier system, which was based largely on the resources of single families or communities. In effect, better insurance has been gained at the cost of diminished flexibility.

Canada's system, dominated as it is by age-conditioned transfers such as OAS, also differs markedly from the primarily earnings-related systems of most other countries, including the

---

7 Elsewhere (Burbidge 1987), I have compared and contrasted the earlier system with the modern one.

United States. This difference is related to the extent of decentralization in the Canadian federation. Since the introduction of the CPP required cooperation between the federal and provincial governments, as do ongoing changes, the transaction costs of changing such an earnings-related scheme are higher in Canada than they are in the United States. Thus, it is hardly surprising that the GIS, which was supposed to be only transitory until the CPP and QPP were established, has proven to be so durable or that certain problems, such as the central one of poverty among elderly single people, have been attacked through increases in the GIS rather than in CPP retirement benefits.

Effects of Current Programs

This section summarizes some of what economists have had to say about the effects of public pension programs.

Most economic analysis presumes full employment of all resources, including labor and physical capital. In this setting, the effects of any change in government policy naturally divide into those on the supply of labor and those on the demand for labor. Effects on the demand for labor operate primarily through changing the stock of physical capital. With more capital, workers can be more productive, which makes them more attractive to employers. Effects on the stock of capital subdivide into effects on investment and effects on saving. Since, in most public pension models, it is assumed that saving governs investment, analysis focuses on saving and tends to ignore effects on investment. Accordingly, the following sections deal with the effects of public pension programs on the labor supply and on saving.

Introductory Remarks

Public pensions transfer resources from the working-age population to those who are elderly or disabled; payroll and income tax revenues, together with some of the increase in government debt, equal the costs of OAS, the GIS, the SPA, and the CPP, period by period. There is no such thing as the effects of an increase in payroll tax rates; the effects depend on what is done with the tax revenue. Effects on the labor supply, for example, will depend on whether retirement pensions or disability benefits or something else is altered. Thus, in defining the question, one must be clear as to how public and private budget constraints are changed.

A second and related point is that one must pay attention to the behavior of all those affected by a change in the program. For example, some of the literature on the saving effects of public pensions, which I discuss below, proceeds as if it were possible to deduce the effects on aggregate savings by studying the saving response of only those of working age. Some economists argue that, if the young save less in response to an expansion of social security, this must imply a decrease in aggregate savings. This is not the case, however — if the young save less and the old *dis*save less, aggregate savings may be unchanged. Aggregate effects depend on how *everyone* reacts to the change in the program.

A third point is that individuals' expectations may play an important role in the effects of changes in public pensions. For example, suppose payroll tax rates were increased to finance an increase in public pensions. If those currently of working age believed that they, too, would receive more generous public pensions on retirement, they would likely reduce their current consumption by less than if they believed that the increase in benefits to the elderly were only temporary and that they would be unable to collect an increased pension on retirement. Obviously, with the former belief, expected lifetime wealth would be higher, inducing higher current consumption. Thus, a government policy change has different effects depending on the beliefs of the economic agents affected by the change.[8] In the current policy setting, I conjecture that most individuals of working age do not believe that the substantial increase in payroll tax rates they have

---

8 For further demonstration of this point, see Burbidge (1991, 323–337).

recently endured implies larger public pension benefits for them in the future. If this is correct, working-age cohorts will be saving more than if they anticipated larger pension benefits on retirement.

Effects on the Labor Supply

In recent decades, there has been an extraordinary decline in labor force participation rates for older men, as shown in Table 5. Between 1961 and 1993, the proportion of males aged 65 to 69 participating in the labor force dropped from more than half to less than one-fifth, while the participation rate for those aged 55 to 64 declined from nearly 86 percent to less than 61 percent. Participation rates for females, in contrast, have increased sharply, reflected in part in Table 5 by the increase for those aged 55 to 64 from just under 25 percent in 1961 to more than 36 percent in 1993.

How should these numbers be interpreted?[9] It is useful to distinguish two effects of changes in public pension programs on the labor supply. First, such programs may have "wealth effects": when a generation is given more generous pensions without having to pay for them, it finds itself wealthier, and there is strong empirical evidence that wealthier people choose to retire earlier. Second, these programs may have "substitution effects": if pensions are altered so that the payoff to working one more year is reduced, people will retire earlier — if the price of leisure declines, they substitute leisure for work. I mentioned earlier that the combined taxback rate in the GIS, the SPA, and Ontario's GAINS program is 100 percent (or possibly higher). This is an extreme case, where working more yields no extra income, and thus the substitution effect implies complete retirement.

---

9 Public finance textbooks often use a consumption-leisure diagram to explain the effects of taxes and transfers derived from a single-period model. Burbidge and Robb (1980) show how one can adapt this framework to interpret the effects of public pension changes derived from a continuous time life-cycle model. The analysis in this section employs this framework. Gustman and Steinmeier (1986) have a more elaborate model of retirement as a two-step process from full-time work to part-time work to complete retirement.

Table 5: ***Labor Force Participation Rates of
Older Males and Females, Selected Years 1961–93***

	Participation Rate for Males Aged:			Participation Rate for Females Aged:		
	55–64	**65–69**	**70 +**	**55–64**	**65–69**	**70 +**
			(percent)			
1961	85.9	50.4	22.0	24.6	10.8	3.8
1965	85.6	46.0	18.1	28.6	12.4	3.4
1970	83.6	37.5	16.3	31.6	10.3	2.9
1975	79.3	29.9	11.0	30.8	9.6	2.3
1976	76.7	25.4	9.8	31.9	7.8	2.2
1977	76.4	25.1	9.2	32.1	8.5	2.0
1978	76.6	23.5	9.6	32.7	7.9	2.7
1979	76.4	24.4	9.1	34.0	8.2	1.9
1980	76.2	23.5	8.9	33.7	8.3	2.1
1981	75.1	21.9	8.9	33.7	7.9	2.5
1982	73.6	22.6	8.3	33.8	8.2	2.1
1983	72.3	21.2	7.9	33.5	7.1	2.7
1984	71.1	20.2	8.1	33.3	7.6	2.5
1985	70.1	19.6	8.0	33.8	8.0	2.3
1986	68.5	18.5	7.6	33.4	7.1	1.9
1987	66.5	19.0	7.4	35.0	6.9	1.8
1988	66.6	18.1	7.2	35.5	7.2	2.2
1989	66.2	16.9	7.1	34.4	7.5	2.1
1990	64.9	18.1	7.2	35.7	7.3	2.0
1991	62.5	17.6	7.5	35.7	7.0	1.7
1992	62.0	18.3	6.4	36.4	7.7	1.5
1993	60.9	16.6	6.4	36.4	7.7	1.8

Source: Statistics Canada, CANSIM database.

One consistent theme in the retirement literature has been that changes in public pensions alone cannot account for the massive decrease in average age at retirement which has been observed in Canada and many other countries for males (see Fields and Mitchell 1984). It is true that expanded intergenerational transfers to elderly Canadians have made them wealthier over the past 35 years at the same time as increases in income, payroll, and taxback rates have reduced the incentive to work. Yet it is changes in *private* pension plans, in which about half the labor force participates, that may explain much of the component of retirement behavior left unaccounted for by changes in public pensions. As the baby boom generation entered the labor force, driving down the wages of younger workers relative to those of older workers, firms discovered a strong incentive to substitute lower-wage younger workers for higher-wage older workers. At the same time, many private pension plans were changed to reduce the reward for working longer, which induced a substitution effect in favor of earlier retirement.

It is worth noting, however, that not all changes over this period worked in the direction of encouraging earlier retirement. Recall, for example, that during the ten-year phase-in period of the CPP, the "0.25" in the formula grew from 0.025 in 1967 to 0.05 in 1968, reaching 0.25 only in 1976. More important, before YMPE caught up to the average industrial wage in 1986, it was rising at 12.5 percent per annum. These rules increased the incentive to work, thereby creating an incentive to delay retirement.[10] With the generosity of pensions increasing so quickly, working even a short while longer caused a sharp increase in

---

10 One might think that the increase in CPP benefits by 0.5 percent for each month that retirement is delayed between ages 60 and 70 would cause people to postpone their decision to retire for as long as possible. Closer inspection of the rules reveals, however, that one may experience low earnings, say, at age 59, begin to collect CPP benefits at age 60, then subsequently return to full-time work at age 61. This means that the 0.5 percent per month rule generates wealth effects that may encourage earlier retirement. In particular, workers with high discount rates (low life expectancies) are quite likely to retire earlier with the 0.5 percent rule in place (see Burbidge 1987, 89–90).

retirement income. In addition, for those with private pensions, most of which are not indexed to inflation, there were times during the 1970s and 1980s when nominal wages were rising rapidly. Given typical defined-benefit private pension formulas, which in these circumstances are so dependent on earnings in the last few years preceding retirement, retiring one year later could entitle one to a much higher real pension. Once again, this implies an incentive to delay retirement.

It may be that, as baby boomers near age 60 and in the absence of a long queue of younger workers awaiting their jobs, firms may rearrange their private pension plans to encourage later retirement. Thus, some of the concern about the future high projected costs of caring for the elderly may be misplaced.

Effects on Saving

In a famous 1974 essay, Feldstein argued that the expansion of the social security system in the United States had discouraged private saving, which had led to a reduction in investment, and, over time, in the country's capital stock. Since Feldstein and many other public finance economists believe that a reduction in the capital stock reduces attainable consumption levels and thus well-being, his essay represented a major attack on social security. Put somewhat differently, he was saying that, while society might still want to have the social security system for reasons of intergenerational equity, the associated welfare costs in terms of slower economic growth were much larger than earlier research would have led one to expect.

The theoretical underpinning for Feldstein's assertion is the life-cycle growth model. Think of the 60 years between ages 21 and 80 as comprising two phases of the life cycle: a 40-year working phase when earnings exceed consumption and wealth is accumulated, followed by a 20-year retirement phase over which consumption is financed out of previously accumulated wealth. In the simple forms of this life-cycle model, the date of death is certain and wealth at death is zero. Thus, an increase in taxes on the young to pay for higher public pensions for the elderly transfers purchasing power from those who are saving to those who are dissaving; therefore, aggregate saving must diminish. Since "saving" is "investment" in this model — where the government's budget is balanced and there is no international trade; more on this presently — the reduction in saving implies a reduction in investment and thus the capital stock.

Since the publication of Feldstein's essay, an enormous literature has developed that explores the relationships between saving and social security and other determinants of saving (see, for example, King 1983; Kotlikoff 1984; and Poterba 1994). There is no consensus on why people save nor, given the quality of the data, is one likely to emerge soon. The possibilities run the gamut from Feldstein's view of large social security effects on aggregate saving to *no* effects — the argument of another famous essay, by Barro, published in the same year (1974) and journal as Feldstein's.

Barro worked within the same framework as Feldstein, but he assumed that the different generations of each family were linked by altruism. In effect, Barro asked how the elderly managed to survive before the existence of social security. If they had depended on private transfers from young to old, the effect of the introduction of government-mandated transfers may simply have been to reduce private transfers. Consider the following example. Suppose, before the advent of social security, a child had planned to give her parents $1,000 per annum during their retirement years. Then suppose that, on introducing social security, the government had taxed the child $600 and distributed that money to the elderly. In Barro's model, the child would simply have cut her parental contribution to $400. In other words the private offset matches the public transfer dollar for dollar, leaving the consumption level of both young and old unchanged, implying that changes in social security have no effects on resource allocations in the economy.[11]

---

11 If taxes exceed the child's parental transfer, the direction of intergenerational transfers switches — parents leave bequests to their children — but the result is the same; the allocation of resources is unaffected.

In a 1987 paper, I reviewed the Canadian and US literature on the saving and labor supply effects of social security. Since then, more work has been done with data on Canadian households. Many of the lower-income elderly are women; *a priori* one would expect this group to be the most likely to consume whatever resources it was given in an attempt to maintain consumption levels. In a 1990 paper, I studied the behavior of elderly women in urban Ontario centers and found that, while many of them had low incomes, they also had low consumption levels; in fact, many of them were still saving many years into retirement. My guess is that consumption declines as health declines (see Robb and Burbidge 1989; and Robb, Magee and Burbidge 1992). More recently, Davies and I (see Burbidge and Davies 1994b) studied the work, consumption, saving and wealth-holding behavior of all Canadian households using Statistics Canada's Family Expenditure Survey and Survey of Consumer Finances over the 1977–90 period. Among other things, we found that the saving rate does not vary much with age; if anything, it *increases* slightly with age — that is, older Canadian households actually save slightly more of their income than do younger households. At the very least, these studies question the argument that changes in public pension plans over the postwar period have caused a major reduction in private saving.

Summary

What effects have changes in Canada's system of public pensions had over the past 30 years? And when significant effects occurred, did they cause declines in well-being?

With regard to effects on retirement, the postwar expansion in social security no doubt contributed, perhaps significantly, to a decline in age at retirement. Moreover, given the baby boom generation and increases in real incomes during the 1945–73 period, a decline in age at retirement constituted a move in the direction of improving well-being. With regard to effects on aggregate saving, a revenue-neutral expansion of public pensions probably does not reduce aggregate saving much, because those paying the taxes and those receiving the transfers probably do not have dramatically different saving rates out of disposable income.[12]

This leaves the question: What are the effects on economic efficiency of using debt (especially since 1973) to finance some of the increase in public pensions? In an open economy such as Canada's, domestic saving may move independently of domestic investment, which depends largely on the world rate of interest. Nevertheless, as many others have observed, a larger Canadian government deficit, given the level of domestic saving, implies larger foreign borrowing and higher foreign interest payments in the future. This drain on the incomes of future generations, as many Canadians can now see clearly, represents a significant loss in well-being.[13]

Pension Policy

In this section, I continue to develop the factual argument which I interpret as support for the first theme of this paper — namely, that, in the long term the feasible size of intergenerational transfers is smaller than it was 20 years ago. I then make two suggestions to help focus debate on the second theme of this paper — that public assistance for the elderly should be tied more closely to the well-being of those whose taxes cover the cost of public pensions.

Table 6 uses the Survey of Consumer Finances (SCF) for 1977, 1984, and 1990 to indicate the components of pre-tax

---

12 This presumes that the programs do not distort relative prices so much that the loss in real income induces a significant reduction in saving.

13 The Barro model is awkward in a small open economy setting because the domestic interest rate is tied to both the family's rate of time preference and the foreign interest rate, and these would almost certainly never be equal. This defect in the Barro model is discussed a greater length in Blanchard and Fischer (1989, chap. 2); and Burbidge and Scarth (1993).

Table 6: **Components of Pre-Tax Annual Incomes for Urban Married-Couple Families with Husband Retired, 1976, 1983, and 1989**

	1976	1983	1989
	(mean amounts in 1990 dollars, unless otherwise specified)		
Average age	70.2	69.8	69.7
Type of income			
Earnings	5,000	4,692	6,532
Share (%)	*20.9*	*16.5*	*17.7*
Investment income	4,474	5,780	6,943
Share (%)	*18.7*	*20.3*	*18.8*
OAS and GIS	7,346	7,889	7,825
Share (%)	*30.7*	*27.7*	*21.2*
CPP/QPP	1,866	3,803	5,803
Share (%)	*7.8*	*13.4*	*15.7*
Pensions and annuities	4,358	4,507	8,013
Share (%)	*18.2*	*15.8*	*21.7*
Other income	902	1,770	1,781
Share (%)	*3.7*	*6.3*	*4.9*
Total	23,946	28,441	36,897

Source: Statistics Canada, Survey of Consumer Finances, 1977, 1984, and 1990, as reported in Burbidge and Davies 1992, table 2.8.

annual incomes for urban married-couple families in which the husband was retired and at least 65 years old. "Earnings" may arise from the participation of wives or other family members in the labor market or from self-employment. "Investment income" excludes anything having to do with RRSPs; all such income is included in "pensions and annuities." "Other income" includes provincial income supplements such as Ontario's GAINS. The numbers reveal a trend toward an increasing reliance on the CPP/QPP, pensions and annuities, and other income; little trend in investment income; and a decreasing reliance on earnings and OAS and the GIS. Most striking is the nearly 50 percent increase in real family income between 1976 and 1989.

Tables 7 and 8 present Statistics Canada estimates of weekly earnings for full-time, full-year male and female workers, aged 23 to 60, by level of education.[14] What is most striking here is that real earnings have been nearly constant for women but that they have been falling for men since the late 1970s. It is worth emphasizing, however, that these are earnings gross of income taxes; as Burbidge and Davies (1994a) show, since income tax rates trended upward during the 1980s, earnings *after* taxes declined for both women and men.

Figure 1, which plots several real income series taken from the tables in this essay, reveals a marked contrast in the real growth rates of various components of the incomes of elderly households and younger men and women. It is instructive to look more carefully at the sources of income for the elderly. Table 6 shows that average family OAS/GIS receipts rose by about $540 per annum between 1976 and 1983 and then were virtually constant between 1983 and 1989. Looking back at Table 1, one can see that this resulted from a sharp increase in maximum GIS payments between 1975 and 1983; since 1983, the maximum OAS/GIS for married couples has been nearly constant (and, after 1985, it was also constant for single individuals).

---

14 All employees are included whether they are paid by salary or otherwise. The SCF reports annual earning for the previous calendar year as well as weeks worked, so one can calculate weekly earnings. The only information available for the previous calendar year on hours worked is the answer to the question, "When you worked, did you typically work 30 or more hours per week or less than 30 hours per week?" The numbers reported here are for "full-time" workers — that is, those claiming to have worked 30 or more hours per week, which is the category that dominates the alternative for both men and women. "Full year" means the individual worked 52 weeks, including holidays.

Figure 1: *Real Growth Rates of Various Income Components, 1971–93*

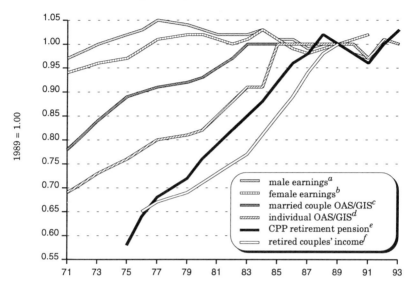

Sources:

[a] Average weekly earnings of full-time, full-year male workers, from Table 7, averaged over all education categories.

[b] Average weekly earnings of full-time, full-year female workers, from Table 8, averaged over all education categories.

[c] Maximum pensions of married couples from the last column of Table 1.

[d] Maximum pensions of individuals from the second-to-last column of Table 1.

[e] Maximum monthly CPP retirement pension from the fifth column of Table 3.

[f] Pre-tax annual incomes of urban married-couple families where the husband is retired, from Table 6.

Returning to Table 6, note that average family CPP/QPP receipts doubled between 1976 and 1983 and then rose by another 50 percent between 1983 and 1989. Looking back at the lower half of Table 3, one sees that YMPE grew by about 45 percent between 1975 and 1985, which boosted the various CPP benefits. In addition, as noted above, disability pensions were raised by $150 per month on April 1, 1987. Increasing labor force partici-

Table 7: *Education and Earnings of Full-Time, Full-Year Male Workers, Selected Years 1971–91*

	Percent in Education Category	Mean Age	Weekly Earnings		
			Mean	Standard Deviation	Median
	(%)		*(1991 dollars)*		
		Elementary Education			
1971	54	41	618	271	577
1973	53	41	654	272	577
1975	36	42	678	292	630
1977	36	43	704	282	662
1979	33	43	695	284	661
1981	29	44	677	274	635
1982	27	44	661	268	638
1984	26	43	672	264	657
1985	24	44	659	285	632
1986	23	44	661	269	651
1987	22	43	674	291	634
1988	21	44	678	300	648
1989	18	44	658	292	639
1990	16	44	669	321	609
1991	15	44	640	279	601
		11–13 Years of Education			
1971	19	38	720	301	685
1973	19	38	766	336	715
1975	26	38	776	339	725
1977	28	38	793	353	749
1979	32	38	773	312	748
1981	32	37	744	299	709
1982	32	37	741	453	710
1984	32	38	729	313	714
1985	33	37	726	317	706
1986	34	37	710	308	680
1987	33	38	724	348	693
1988	34	38	732	332	675
1989	39	38	728	326	703
1990	40	38	745	346	675
1991	41	38	703	310	673

Table 7 - continued

	% in Education Category	Mean Age	Weekly Earnings		
			Mean	Standard Deviation	Median
	(%)			*(1991 dollars)*	
		Some Postsecondary Education			
1971	16	38	792	374	715
1973	17	37	814	381	742
1975	22	37	808	360	747
1977	22	37	820	337	767
1979	20	36	817	359	756
1981	22	36	789	316	748
1982	23	37	787	340	742
1984	23	36	771	319	762
1985	24	36	775	321	750
1986	24	36	773	361	728
1987	25	37	769	352	723
1988	26	37	796	386	726
1989	25	37	760	358	703
1990	25	38	792	391	719
1991	24	38	766	337	721
		University Degree			
1971	11	38	1,063	652	932
1973	11	38	1,078	549	969
1975	16	37	1,073	535	954
1977	14	37	1,024	433	976
1979	15	38	1,048	515	955
1981	16	38	1,029	441	968
1982	18	39	1,031	477	950
1984	19	39	1,015	421	960
1985	19	39	1,006	443	935
1986	19	39	1,022	454	967
1987	20	39	1,014	554	928
1988	19	39	1,008	504	931
1989	18	39	1,041	495	948
1990	19	39	1,022	554	931
1991	20	40	1,038	559	923

Source: Author's calculations, using Statistics Canada's Survey of Consumer Finances public use microdata tapes.

Table 8:   *Education and Earnings of Full-Time,*
Full-Year Female Workers, Selected Years 1971–91

	Percent in Education Category	Mean Age	Weekly Earnings		
			Mean	Standard Deviation	Median
	(%)		*(1991 dollars)*		
	Elementary Education				
1971	44	41	338	205	307
1973	41	41	353	143	327
1975	27	42	365	137	343
1977	26	42	392	186	364
1979	24	42	385	168	360
1981	22	43	386	166	354
1982	21	43	382	163	357
1984	18	44	375	164	360
1985	17	43	377	173	355
1986	15	42	389	193	338
1987	16	43	384	180	343
1988	15	43	380	174	355
1989	14	44	372	174	354
1990	12	44	392	174	348
1991	10	44	396	189	354
	11–13 Years of Education				
1971	26	36	411	140	388
1973	25	37	445	155	409
1975	33	37	451	165	424
1977	36	37	457	187	431
1979	40	37	473	182	446
1981	38	36	465	198	429
1982	37	36	449	183	418
1984	37	36	459	191	447
1985	38	36	442	195	425
1986	38	37	453	203	430
1987	36	37	458	209	422
1988	36	37	454	205	409
1989	41	37	453	199	425
1990	41	37	471	208	427
1991	42	38	466	194	442

Table 8 - continued

	% in Education Category	Mean Age	Weekly Earnings		
			Mean	**Standard Deviation**	**Median**
	(%)		*(1991 dollars)*		
	Some Postsecondary Education				
1971	23	37	531	263	493
1973	25	36	530	198	485
1975	28	35	535	215	490
1977	25	36	534	220	492
1979	23	35	530	218	483
1981	27	35	521	216	473
1982	26	35	522	208	484
1984	27	35	523	214	485
1985	29	36	519	233	483
1986	29	36	519	213	479
1987	30	36	515	225	450
1988	30	35	511	213	464
1989	30	36	511	224	463
1990	31	37	546	225	496
1991	31	37	539	234	481
	University Degree				
1971	8	36	718	292	660
1973	8	35	698	253	674
1975	12	34	688	265	661
1977	12	35	714	307	710
1979	12	36	740	299	711
1981	13	35	734	282	733
1982	15	35	721	267	711
1984	17	36	722	290	731
1985	17	37	725	290	717
1986	18	36	722	330	700
1987	19	36	739	306	706
1988	19	37	748	346	720
1989	16	37	764	319	728
1990	16	37	753	344	722
1991	17	38	769	315	736

Source: Author's calculations, using Statistics Canada's Survey of Consumer Finances public use microdata tapes.

pation rates for women also contributed to the remarkable increase in CPP/QPP benefits documented in Table 6.

Although it is clear from Table 6 that real earnings and real investment income grew sharply between 1983 and 1989, real pension and annuity income grew by over 75 percent. While the numbers do not permit one to break this down into increases in registered pension plan (RPP) benefits and RRSPs, we do know that RPPs were not growing in importance over this period while RRSPs had been and continued to be an ever more popular savings vehicle between the mid-1970s and now. "Revenue losses" from the favorable treatment accorded RPPs and RRSPs were estimated at 25 to 30 percent of federal government revenue in 1989 (see Burbidge and Davies 1994b).[15] Finally, one should not underestimate the effects of higher real interest rates during the 1980s, which, among other things, redistributed wealth away from young, mortgage-holding families to the investment-holding elderly.

And so, for a variety of reasons, real transfers to elderly households continued to increase long after real earnings for both men and women of working age stagnated as a consequence of slower rates of real growth after 1973. These transfers have been financed by increasing tax rates and by issuing debt, neither of which is sustainable indefinitely. To re-emphasize my themes, 1970s' levels of per capita intergenerational transfers are simply unfeasible in Canada today. Government-mandated intergenerational transfers to the elderly should be brought into line with what working-age generations can afford and wish to provide.

In an earlier review of several of the many pension reform documents (Burbidge 1987), I judged that none of them adequately dealt with Canada's public pension problem, nor do any

---

15 The *Financial Post* (November 18, 1994, p. 3) reported that the minister of finance estimates Ottawa forgoes $14.9 billion of tax revenues because of tax-sheltered retirement savings, but that many question this estimate because it makes no allowance for the taxes that will be collected when funds are withdrawn from RRSPs.

of the suggestions that have appeared more recently. It is obvious that, in Canada and many other countries, citizens and their governments view poverty in old age differently from poverty among prime-age males and females. (How societies trade off poverty between the elderly and children is more controversial.) Given the preferences many societies apparently reveal, it would appear that, if reductions in intergenerational transfers to the elderly are to be implemented, the social safety net for low-income elderly will be protected and cuts will begin with the benefits payable to middle- and higher-income individuals. This is already evident in the social benefits repayment line of Canada's personal income tax form, whereby the higher-income elderly repay all or part of their OAS receipts. This logic implies that cuts will be made either to the RRSP system or to the CPP. Since the main rationale for the significant expansion of RRSP limits over the past ten years was to level the playing field between those whose jobs had registered pension plans and those that did not, it would be unfair to cut back RRSP limits without corresponding cutbacks for RPPs. Given the complexity of changing RPP rules, my view is that the CPP should be the target for change.

I do not have fully articulated reform proposals to put forward at this point since much more work is required to support any particular one. Following, however, are two proposals that may be worth further consideration.

The first is the possibility of phasing out the CPP over a ten-year period. If it is true that the scheduled increases in CPP payroll tax rates will generate enough revenue each year to cover CPP benefits in their current form, a proportional reduction in tax rates and benefits at the rate of, say, 10 percent each year, should still balance the CPP budget on a "pay-as-you-go" footing. I believe that, for many elderly, reduced CPP benefits would be partially replaced by larger GIS payments and by retaining (after income taxes) a larger proportion of OAS benefits. This could be verified by studying existing microdata available from the SCF or by simulating the switch in an already existing model of public pensions. This would, however, imply a larger government deficit. One way to eliminate this problem would be to stagger the CPP benefit and payroll tax reductions starting with benefit reductions in year 1 and no payroll tax reductions until year 2, and then retaining some reduced payroll tax rate to balance the extra OAS/GIS expenditures. Without further research, it is difficult to know what the effects of phasing out the CPP would be. My guess is that it might appeal to younger generations who have been skeptical about the likelihood of receiving CPP benefits by the second and third decades of the twenty-first century and who would welcome the cut in payroll taxes. Middle- and upper-income elderly probably would suffer a loss in real income but they might also choose a phase-out of the CPP over a restriction in RRSPs. The blow for lower-income elderly likely would be cushioned by higher GIS payments and the ability to retain, after taxes, a larger share of OAS.

A second proposal is motivated by the trend shown in Figure 1, particularly by the decade between 1975 and 1985 during which real earnings were stagnating, yet OAS and the GIS continued to grow in real terms. Instead of fixing OAS, GIS, and SPA benefits and trying to raise enough in taxes to cover the costs of these programs, what would happen if the procedure were reversed? Set an OAS/GIS/SPA formula that divides up whatever money is allotted to public pensions and then cap the proportion of government revenue that is paid out each year in public pensions. This proposal would tie intergenerational transfers to the elderly more closely to working generations' ability to pay. Once again, however, much more work is required to understand what the effects of this structural change would be.

References

Barro, R.J. 1974. "Are Government Bonds Net Wealth?" *Journal of Political Economy* 82 (6): 1095–1118.

Blanchard, O.J., and S. Fischer. 1989. *Lectures on Macroeconomics.* Cambridge, Mass.: MIT Press.

Burbidge, J.B. 1987. *Social Security in Canada: An Economic Appraisal.* Canadian Tax Paper 79. Toronto: Canadian Tax Foundation.

———. 1990. "Pension Reform and Elderly Women: Some Evidence for Ontario Urban Centres." In A. Asimakopulos, R. Cairns, and C. Green, eds., *Economic Theory, Welfare and the State.* London: Macmillan.

———. 1991. "Social Security and Public Debt in Historical Perspective." In L. Eden, ed., *Retrospectives on Public Finance.* Fiscal Reform in the Developing World Series. Durham, NC: Duke University Press.

———, and J.B. Davies. 1994a. "Government Incentives and Household Saving in Canada." In J.M. Poterba, ed., *Public Policies and Household Saving.* Chicago: University of Chicago Press for the National Bureau of Economic Research.

———, and J.B. Davies. 1994b. "Household Data on Saving Behaviour in Canada." In J.M. Poterba, ed., *International Comparisons of Household Saving.* Chicago: University of Chicago Press for the National Bureau of Economic Research.

———, and A.L. Robb. 1980. "Pensions and Retirement Behaviour." *Canadian Journal of Economics* 13 (August): 421–437.

———, and W.M. Scarth, 1993. "Eliminating Interest Taxation and Tariffs: The Underpinnings for Recent Canadian Policy." *Canadian Journal of Economics.* Forthcoming.

CTF (Canadian Tax Foundation). 1993. *The National Finances.* Toronto: Canadian Tax Foundation.

Feldstein, M.S. 1974. "Social Security, Induced Retirement, and Aggregate Capital Accumulation." *Journal of Political Economy* 82 (5): 905–926.

Fields, G.S., and O.S. Mitchell. 1984. *Retirement, Pensions, and Social Security.* Cambridge, Mass.: MIT Press.

Gustman, A.L., and T.L. Steinmeier. 1986. "A Structural Retirement Model." *Econometrica* 54 (3): 555–584.

King, M.A. 1983. *The Economics of Saving*. NBER Working Paper 1247. Cambridge, Mass.: National Bureau of Economic Research.

Kotlikoff, L.J. 1984. "Taxation and Savings: A Neoclassical Perspective." *Journal of Economic Literature* 22 (4): 1576–1629.

Poterba, J.M., ed. 1994. *Public Policies and Household Saving*. Chicago: University of Chicago Press for the National Bureau of Economic Research.

Robb, A.L., and J.B. Burbidge. 1989. "Consumption, Income and Retirement." *Canadian Journal of Economics* 22 (August): 522–542.

———, L. Magee, and J.B. Burbidge. 1992. "Kernel Smoothed Consumption-Age Quantiles." *Canadian Journal of Economics* 25 (August): 669–680.

Restoring the Canada Pension Plan:
Simulating the Future and Stimulating the Social Policy Debate

Newman Lam,
Michael J. Prince, and James Cutt

All over the globe, issues of retirement and pension schemes are pressing on governments' agendas as policy advisers and decisionmakers are engaged in what a recent World Bank report calls *Averting the Old Age Crisis*.

In Canada, the last national pension debate (in the late 1970s and 1980s) stressed improving benefits and introducing new ones. Current discussions, by contrast, emphasize the fiscal limits of the state and the financial distress anticipated for the Canada Pension Plan (CPP) and other old age benefit programs (Prince 1996). Building on previous work (Lam, Prince, and Cutt 1993; Lam, Cutt, and Prince 1995; 1996) we consider here several options for reforming the CPP.

Our position is that the CPP is part of Canada's heritage that is worth keeping but needs prompt renovation. Demographic forces plus a number of policy-driven factors are reducing revenues to and increasing expenditures by the plan, leaving it in such poor fiscal health that Canadians must be bold in contemplating options for change. Fairly simple corrective measures do exist, however, and if instituted soon they could save the plan without inequity to the workers or the retirees of today and of the future.

The paper is organized into five main sections. The first describes the nature of the CPP and the way it operates.[1] The second considers the causes of the CPP's financial problems: the much discussed rise in the average age of the population and several design factors that have contributed to the fiscal weakness of the plan. The next and longest part surveys a number of options for reform, examining their rationales, their effects on contributors, and their socio-legal implications; for many, we also consider the financial impact, reporting the results of computer-based simulations. Finally, we recommend a series of measures to implement for reforming the CPP. An appendix describes our basic calculations for deriving the data required for the simulations.

How the CPP Works

Before attempting to improve anything, the wise mechanic reviews the way it works now. The same is (or should be) true for policymakers.[2]

The CPP is one of Canada's basic and most cherished programs for ensuring that elderly people have funds to live on during their retirement. Technically, it is a *defined benefits pension scheme.* That is, a contributor receives an entitlement to benefits that are predefined (actually, defined annually by the federal government) and that do not have a direct or strong link to that individual's contributions. (In contrast, what is called an *actuarially fair pension scheme* — the kind common in the private sector — provides a retiree with the capitalized value of his or her contributions.)

---

1 Some readers are undoubtedly familiar with this material, which emphasizes basic terminology, and calculation methods. They may wish to skip to the next section.

2 The following section is based on Lam (1993, 42–44).

CPP Eligibility and Contributions

CPP coverage is mandatory for virtually all paid members of the Canadian labor force — both employees and the self-employed — between ages 18 and 70. The only workers not included are

- Quebec residents, who are covered by the Quebec Pension Plan (QPP); members of the Canadian Forces and the Royal Canadian Mounted Police residing in Quebec are, however, covered by the CPP;
- individuals who earn less than the year's basic exemption (see below);
- individuals to whom a retirement or disability pension is already payable under the *Canada Pension Plan Act*;
- members of certain religious groups; and
- individuals who are older than age 70.

The contribution to the CPP is made equally by employer and employee.[3] The upper limit is called the *year's maximum pensionable earnings* (YMPE). This amount is adjusted upward annually in accordance with Statistics Canada's index of industrial wages and salaries (the Average Industrial Wage), rounded to the nearest $100. (If that index decreases, the YMPE is held at its previous level.) The lower limit is called the *year's basic exemption (YBE)*. It is 10 percent of the YMPE, rounded to the nearest $100.

The amount of an individual's *contributory earnings*, the earnings on which the CPP contribution is determined is calculated by subtracting the YBE from *pensionable earnings*, which are the lesser of annual earnings or the YMPE.

The CPP contribution is calculated by multiplying contributory earnings by a universal contribution rate. In 1996, an employee is required to contribute 2.8 percent of contributory earnings

---

3 The amount of that contribution is based on the individual's earnings between an upper and a lower limit. Self-employed workers pay both the employer's and the employee's contribution.

to the CPP, with the employer providing an equal amount. The total *contribution rate* is thus 5.6 percent of contributory earnings. According to the *Canada Pension Plan Fifteenth Statutory Actuarial Report* (Canada 1995b), the contribution rate is expected to increase by 0.2 of a percentage point or more annually until 2030.

Retirement Pensions

The size of the CPP retirement pension is based largely on the YMPE before retirement. The starting amount is equal to 25 percent of the average YMPE for the three years before retirement (including the year in which the contributor retires) multiplied by the average earnings ratio, which is calculated as follows.

The starting point is the *earnings ratio*, which is monthly pensionable earnings divided by one-twelfth of the applicable YMPE. The *average earnings ratio* is then calculated by averaging the earnings ratios over the entire contributory period.

The *contributory period* is the time period from which contributions begin to the time of retirement less any periods during which no contributions are made for the individual. Excluded from the contributory period may be periods of low earnings that fall under the following categories:

- any period in which the individual has at least one child less than 7 years of age;
- any period after the age of 65 and before retirement commences;
- after the time periods specified in the previous two points have been deducted, 15 percent of the months remaining in the contributory period.

The contributory period cannot be reduced to less than 120 months (ten years). The contributory period is reduced only if the reduction will improve the average earnings ratio.

If a person elects to retire before age 65, the CPP pension is reduced by 0.5 percent for each month of early retirement. If a person chooses to postpone retirement after age 65, the pension is increased by 0.5 percent for each month of postponed retirement.

The CPP pension is adjusted upward annually according to the consumer price index (CPI). If the adjustment results in a decrease in pension, the amount is held at the level of the previous year.

CPP Financing

The CPP has two — and only two — sources of revenue: contributions and returns from its general Investment Fund. Its expenses are considerable.

The plan is run as a pay-as-you-go (PAYGO) system, which means that current contributions are first used to pay current benefits and operating expenses. An amount equal to the estimated expenditures of the next three months is always held in reserve. Anything remaining is added to the CPP Investment Fund to generate revenues. The fund is limited to purchasing securities of the provinces in proportion to the contributions made by the residents of each.[4] The term of maturity of the securities must be 20 years or less (20 years is the standard, because long-term securities, under normal economic conditions, provide more stable and higher yields than short-term ones). If the CPP has a cash shortfall, the minister of finance has the authority to redeem provincial securities before their maturity to meet payments.[5]

The CPP currently owes contributors, past and present, a huge unfunded liability.[6] The amount was estimated at $556 billion at the end of 1995, and, under the current schedule of contribution rates, it would grow by $50 billion a year (Federal,

---

4 This arrangement was part of the federal-provincial deal struck when the CPP was instituted in 1966. The availability of the fund has become important to the finances of all the provinces except Quebec.

5 This authority has never been used.

6 For employer-sponsored pension plans, actuaries calculate the value of the fund that must be set aside to pay for all the benefits promised by the plan to its current contributors and recipients. The shortfall between the plan's assets and the value of all its promises is called an *unfunded liability*.

Provincial, and Territorial Governments of Canada 1996). In other words, if the CPP were to be changed into a fully funded system today, it would owe current contributors and benefit recipients $556 billion of promised payments after liquidating all its assets.

An Overview

In terms of social welfare, the CPP offers a number of attractive features, such as pension indexation and benefits for surviving spouses and disabled workers. Since the plan is self-financed, these features are financed by redistributing funds from one group of contributors to another. Those who have contributed more do not necessarily receive a proportional increase in benefits. Contributions into the CPP, are thus, in essence a dedicated tax.

The CPP is clearly related to other federal support programs, such as the Old Age Security (OAS), Guaranteed Income Supplement (GIS),[7] and Spouses' Allowance (SPA), but it is distinct in a number of ways. First, the CPP pays benefits only to individuals who have contributed to the plan (and their family members), whereas everyone who qualifies is entitled to receive the OAS, GIS, and SPA. Second, all CPP contributions must be spent on the plan while the general tax revenues used for the other programs are not restricted to one purpose. Third, the OAS, GIS, and SPA do not owe any liability to taxpayers and can be eliminated at any time. The CPP, on the contrary, is a contributory plan that in principle owes defined benefits to contributors and could be morally and legally difficult to terminate without their consent. Overall, the Canadian institution that is the CPP is a social insurance program involving compulsory participation for all but a relatively few adults in a process of present and deferred consumption via intergenerational redistribution. As an established and accepted arrangement for planning for and producing

---

7 Recall that the OAS and GIS will be combined to form the new Seniors Benefit in 2001.

retirement income, it is a social contract across generations (Lam, Cutt, and Prince 1996), demanding that Canadians decide what the balance should be between present and future generations.

It is also a *federalized* social contract (Doern, Maslove, and Prince 1988), a major intergovernmental program that is a political pact between Ottawa and the provincial governments and that constitutes a complex web of obligations and entitlements.

The Problem and Its Causes

Despite the CPP's popularity and obvious benefits for social welfare, the question today is its future sustainability. What must be done to ensure that retired Canadians continue to have protection from penury in old age?

Answering that question requires understanding the causes of the problem. The popular belief is that the CPP's anticipated financial difficulties are the result of profound changes in the population profile over the postwar decades. Media reports, everyday conversations, and even some policy analyses refer to the plan as sitting on a demographic time bomb, given the rising average age of Canadian society. There are dire predictions of fundamental shifts in senior-to-worker dependency ratios and of consequent intergenerational political clashes as silver-haired baby boomers and harried members of generation X battle over pension benefits for the next 20 or 30 years.

Given this perspective, demographic aging has become a guiding paradigm in thinking about pensions (and other programs) in the Canadian welfare state (McDaniel 1987). Indeed, the official discourse on pension reform, as expressed by the budgets of the Chrétien government, emphasizes the cost concerns of an aging population and the fiscal sustainability of federal programs for the elderly (Prince 1996).

Unquestionably, Canada does face a rise in the proportion of its population that is over age 65, and the shift does have serious implications for the CPP. But that challenge is not the only reason for the plan's financial problems. They are, in fact, caused by a number of factors that have reduced revenues and increased expenditures. These factors include the low contribution rate, low returns on CPP investments, increased CPP benefits, rapid increases in the upper limit on pensionable earnings (the YMPE), and the short contributory period for entitlement to a full pension. In this section, we examine each of these factors, starting with the shifting demographic situation.

The Baby Boom and the Baby Bust

Because a PAYGO system pays as it receives, it runs into financial difficulties when revenues and expenses fluctuate in opposite directions. This is exactly what has been happening to the CPP.

One reason is that, after World War II, births in some industrialized countries, including Canada, increased suddenly. This baby boom continued until the late 1950s, but since then, the birth rate has been declining steadily. As a result of the boom, the Canadian workforce expanded rapidly in the 1960s and continued to grow as a proportion of the population until the late 1970s. During this period of expansion, CPP revenues easily exceeded expenditures, providing a condition for increasing benefits and maintaining contribution rates at a very low level.

Given the more recent declines in the birth rate, however the expansion has since slowed and, in the early twenty-first century, when the baby boom generation reaches retirement age, the proportion of Canadians of working age will fall. Benefit expenditures will increase while contributions decrease. Without corrective measures, expenditures will exceed revenues and the CPP will accumulate serious deficits.

In brief, this popular view holds that the CPP will encounter negative cash flows[8] in the next century when the baby boom generation reaches retirement age. Yet CPP expenditures began

---

8 Cash flows are defined in the CPP's actuarial reports as contributions less expenditures — in other words, the income from the investment fund is ignored.

Figure 1: *Changes in the CPP Cash Flow, 1967–95*

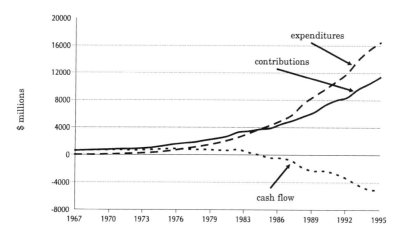

Sources: Canada, Department of Human Resources Development (formerly Department of National Health and Welfare), *Year End Reports of Income Security Programs* (Ottawa), various years; and Canada 1995b.

to exceed contributions in 1984, and the cash flow has been increasingly negative ever since, being projected to reach $4.3 billion in 1995 (see Figure 1). Why do the negative cash flows occur when there is a large workforce to support a relatively small number of benefit recipients?

Setting aside that question for a moment, we ask how the CPP itself views the situation. According to its own projections (Canada 1995b), expenditures will continue to exceed contributions, using up the reserve accumulated over the past 30 years by 2015 (see Figure 2).

The CPP makes this gloomy forecast in spite of proposing steep increases in the contribution rate — raises that would take it to more than 13 percent by 2021 and to more than 15 percent by 2030 (see Figure 3).[9]

---

9 Figure 2 assumes the rate increases of Figure 3 but still shows a negative account balance from 2015 until 2023. The CPP report (Canada 1995b) gives no clear indication how the plan would manage with such a shortfall. It seems reasonable to presume, however, that the CPP would borrow to continue paying promised benefits.

Figure 2: *Projected Changes in the CPP Account, 1996–2025*

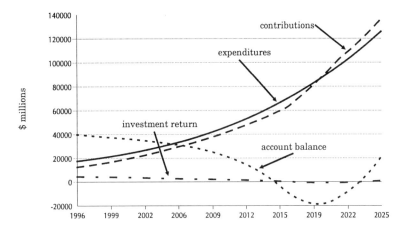

Source: Canada 1995b.

The business community has expressed alarm about such increases. The Board of Trade of Metropolitan Toronto (1993, 1), for example, says that the "schedule of increasing contributions…will eventually place too high a cost burden on employers and future generations of Canadians" and warns that, in light of increasing income and payroll taxes, "there is a reasonable risk that future taxpayers and employers will react in ways which will have adverse consequences for growth, investment and employment in Canada." It is reasonable to assume that young workers and future generations, who have to bear the cost for a long time to come, would also object to such increases.

As already suggested, however, demographic changes provide a quick and dirty explanation — or a convenient excuse — for the CPP's financial problems. Its negative cash flows have been caused by both insufficient revenues and excessive expenditures.

The Contribution Rate

Because a PAYGO system pays as it receives, it can set the initial contribution rate at a very low level when there are few benefit

Figure 3: *Contribution Rates Proposed by the CPP, 1996–2025*

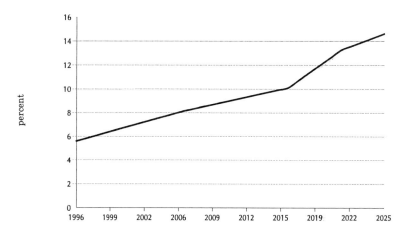

Source: Canada 1995b.

recipients — a feature that makes it *"very attractive to the early participants and thus to the politicians who introduce such a system"* (Brown 1993, 17). As the plan matures and the number of retirees increases, the contribution rate will have to increase in order to maintain the same level of benefits.

When the CPP came into effect in 1966, a time when the workforce was growing rapidly, a 3.6 percent contribution rate was more than sufficient to meet benefit payments. Since then, however, the number of pension recipients has increased, *and* their benefits have been enriched. In 1975, survivor benefits were provided to widowers as well as widows, retirement and earnings tests were dropped for retirement benefits, and all CPP benefits were fully indexed to increases in the CPI.[10] In 1978, the plan introduced a dropout provision to allow certain months of low

---

10 Previously, widowers received survivor benefits only if they were disabled and dependent; contributors ages 65 to 69 could receive retirement benefits only if they passed a retirement test, and their subsequent benefits up to age 70 were reduced if they earned more than a set amount; and there had been a 2 percent ceiling on indexation.

Figure 4:   CPP Contribution Rates, 1967–95

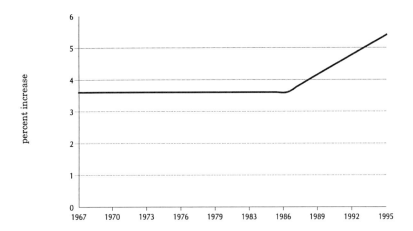

Source: Data provided by Canada, Department of Human Resources Development.

income to be excluded from the pension calculation; the result was higher pension amounts. In 1987, disability benefits were increased, and recipients of survivor benefits were allowed to keep this entitlement on remarriage.

The CPP should have increased the contribution rate to accommodate the higher expenditures that resulted from these changes. For the first 21 years, however, the contribution rate was maintained at the initial level. In 1982, a federal green paper (Canada 1982) recommended reviewing and raising the rate. Yet it was not increased until 1987, five years after the recommendation was made (see Figure 4). Since expenditures began to exceed contributions in 1984, the reluctance to increase the contribution rate is explicable only in political terms.

In brief, the low contribution rate has severely limited CPP revenues.

Return on Investments

The plan's only other source of revenue is the CPP Investment Fund; it invests exclusively in provincial securities, which are low

Figure 5: *Rate of Return on Investment: The CPP and the Investment Fund Industry, 1967–89* [a]

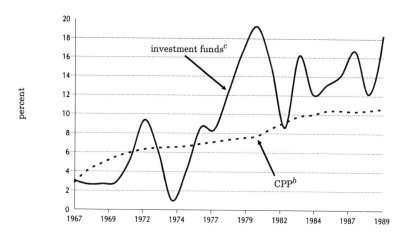

[a] For convenience, we used investment funds data from Statistics Canada; the agency discontinued the series after 1989. Had it been continued, we have no doubt that the spread with the CPP returns would have been at least as great as it is in the last six years shown here.

[b] Calculated as interest income divided by average account balance. Income taxes were ignored.

[c] Calculated as the net income of the industry divided by its average account balance. Corporate income taxes were deducted before calculating the net income of the industry.

Source: CPP data are from Canada, Department of Human Resources Development (formerly Department of National Health and Welfare), *Year End Reports of Income Security Programs* (Ottawa), various years; investment funds data are from Statistics Canada, cat. 61-006.

risk and generally provide returns which are lower than the market average.

A good investment strategy balances risks against returns. A well-diversified portfolio of private and public assets could generate higher yields and still maintain a relatively low level of risk. Figure 5 compares average yields gained by the CPP Investment Fund against net returns from the investment funds industry (whose wide variety of portfolios contain both private and public sector securities). Clearly, the returns on investment funds are less stable but generally higher than the CPP's returns.

Figure 6: *Value of $1 Compounded in the CPP and the Investment Fund Industry, 1967–89*

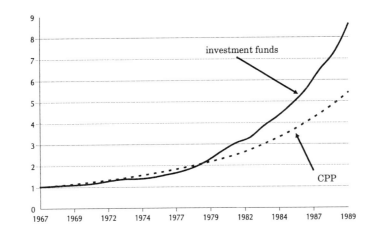

Source: Based on data in Figure 5.

Figure 6 reveals much the same result, calculated a different way: by comparing the compounded values of a dollar from 1967 in the two types of investment. Investment funds had some low yields in the late 1960s and in the mid 1970s, but since 1976, they have consistently had higher yields than the CPP. A dollar placed in the CPP Investment Fund amounted to $5.41 at the end of 1989. The same dollar in investment funds would have amounted to $8.60 over the same time — 59 percent more than in the CPP.

We conclude that, by investing exclusively in provincial securities, the CPP has limited the earnings potential of its investment fund. True that fund has become an important source of capital for the provinces. The CPP's objective, however, is not to finance the provinces — it is to provide a good pension scheme for Canadians.

Benefit Payments

The CPP's primary expenditure is benefit payments, and they have skyrocketed over the years. One reason is the enormous growth in the number of contributors who have retired, but another is the considerable enrichment of benefits, as already described.

Because the CPP is a public pension scheme, it is inherently affected by political agendas. Politicians react to public pressure, which had led them into promising present benefits at the expense of future generations (James 1995). An intergovernmental study (Federal, Provincial, and Territorial Governments of Canada 1996) indicates that a 2.4 percentage point increase in the contribution rate is required to finance the benefit enrichments. From 1987 to 1996, the contribution rate has been increased only two percentage points — a rise insufficient to finance the benefit enrichments, resulting in shortfalls that will need to be offset in the future.[11]

The YMPE

Frequent increases in the YMPE have also led to a higher level of retirement benefit.[12] Recall that the YMPE is adjusted annually, according to the increase in industrial wages and salaries reported by Statistics Canada. During the 1970s and early 1980s, these earnings increased rapidly, causing corresponding rises in the YMPE (see Figure 7). The YMPE increases of more than 10 percent per annum from 1974 to 1986 meant rapid increases in CPP pension expenditure (although they also led to higher contributions). Individuals who retired during that period instantly had higher CPP pensions regardless of whether they had contributed enough to justify the higher benefits. This is, however, the nature of PAYGO systems in which each generation pays the benefits of the previous one.

---

11 In stating that the "benefit enrichments have added a further 2.4 percentage points to the long term costs of the plan" (Federal, Provincial, and Territorial Governments of Canada 1996, 24), the authors of the joint study do not elaborate on when they think the rise on the contribution rate should be (or should have been) instituted or whether they envision it as additional to the two percentage point increase now in place.

12 Because, as explained earlier, the base for calculating the retirement pension is the average YMPE for the three years before retirement.

Figure 7: *Increases in Preretirement*
Income Earnings and YMPE, 1967–95

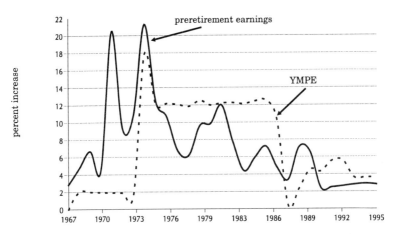

Sources: Canada, Department of Human Resources Development (formerly Department
of National Health and Welfare), *Canada Pension Plan Contributors* and *Year
End Reports of Income Security Programs* (Ottawa), various years;

The Contributory Period

For full pension entitlement, the CPP requires a minimum contributory period of 120 months. Most of the current benefit recipients had more than 10 years but less than 30 years of contributions.

Can a contributory period of less than 30 years be sufficient to finance the current benefits? To answer this question, we compare actuarially fair pensions against CPP retirement pensions for 30 years of continuous contributions from the inception of the program in 1966 to retirement in 1995 (Table 1). Notice the various possible life expectancies.[13] For all that are more than 70 years, the CPP pension is larger than the actuarially based one. Thus, even a full 30 years of contributions is insufficient to

---

13 According to the joint study of the Federal, Provincial, and Territorial Governments of Canada (1996), a Canadian who became 65 in 1995 had an overall life expectancy of 83.4 years.

Table 1:   *Actuarially Based and CPP Pensions for Continuous Contributions from 1966 to Retirement in 1995*

Life Expectancy	Actuarially Based Pensions[a]	CPP Pension	Difference
(age)		*(1995 dollars)*	
70	9,014	8,642	372
75	5,159	8,642	– 3,483
80	3,719	8,642	– 4,923
85	2,968	8,642	– 5,674
90	2,509	8,642	– 6,133

[a] To calculate the actuarially fair pension payments, we compounded the value of the contributions over time; for the retirement period, we assumed the fund balance would continue to compound while being reduced to pay benefits until it was exhausted at the end of the lifespan. We used the actual average earnings of contributors by age group and the actual rates of return on investment, from 1966 to 1995, as reported by the CPP, and assumed a real rate of return of 2 percent for the period after 1995.

Sources: For historical data, Canada, Department of Human Resources Development (formerly Department of National Health and Welfare), *Canada Pension Plan Contributors* and *Year End Reports of Income Security Programs* (Ottawa), various years; for projection data for the period after 1995, Canada 1995a.

finance today's retirement pensions (much less other benefits, such as survivor and disability benefits).

In other words, at existing contribution rates, the contributory period required to support a full pension is much longer than 10 years. Without contribution rate increases, the current contributory period provides insufficient funds for benefit commitments.

Options for Reform

In recent years, discussions on pension policy have generated a number of suggestions for CPP reform, ranging from radical structural changes to modifications of the present system. Structural changes, especially drastic ones, inevitably would involve implementation details that are not yet fully understood, so we concentrate here on ways in which the existing plan could be changed to improve revenues and to reduce costs without losing the universality, portability, and security that are among its attractive features (Canadian Institute of Actuaries 1993).[14] To see the effects of those options that we considered promising, we ran computer simulations based on a person with the average income of all CPP contributors. We assumed that this individual was 21 years of age in 1995 and may retire at age 65 — an average contributor who is going to carry the financial burden of the CPP in the near future. The contributions to be made for this person depend on his or her income during each year of working life and on the corresponding YMPEs, which are set out in Table 2.[15]

We also used a group of basic assumptions that seem realistic but conservative enough to avoid overoptimistic results:

- A 2 percent real rate of investment return. (From 1966 to 1989, the real rate of investment return was 1.5 percent for the CPP and 3.5 percent for market averages — see Figure 5.)
- A life expectancy of 85 years. This figure is slightly higher than the average of 83.6 years projected by the CPP (Canada 1995b) and Statistics Canada (Peron and Strohmenger,

---

14 This focus is not meant to imply that we reject all proposals for structural change. Indeed, we believe that Canadians must be bold and creative in seeking solutions to a serious problem of social welfare. But doing radical reform properly takes time, and the CPP's cash flow is becoming more and more negative every month. Consequently, we urge simultaneously adopting modifications of the current plan and further studying possible structural changes to identify their economic, social, and political implications.

Among the radical proposals we think worth more examination are: running the CPP as a regulated mandatory private pension plan (Chile provides an interesting model — see Hachette and Luders 1993); decentralizing the CPP into a series of regional pension funds (Moscovitch 1993); and rolling the OAS, GIS, and CPP into a single overarching program for the elderly (Courchene 1994).

15 See the appendix for a description of the way we projected the annual incomes and YMPEs. It is worth noting here that we used the rates of earnings increase and of inflation projected by the CPP; significant deviations from these projections will render our results less reliable.

cat. 82-543); we used the longer lifespan to ensure that we did not underestimate the required contribution rate. The shorter the life expectancy, the smaller the number of benefit payments and thus the lower the contribution rate required.

- A contributory period of 40 years. This assumption allows for five years of "idle time" during the working career, time that may be spent in training, childrearing, or looking for work.

The values shown in Table 2 and in the simulation results are in *constant* 1995 dollars to render the results of different simulations comparable.

Raising Revenues

The CPP receives revenue from two sources: contributions paid by employers and employees, and investment returns. There are ways to increase both.

Increasing the Contribution Rate

Increasing the contribution rate, the most direct (though the least innovative) way to increase revenues, is essential because governments maintained the rate at a low level for too long. The rate increases projected by the CPP (Canada 1995b), however, are too steep and will continue for too long a period of time. Many commentators would prefer a long-term rate of 8 percent or less (Board of Trade of Metropolitan Toronto 1993; Lam, Cutt, and Prince 1995; Robson 1996). Surely the contribution rate has to be kept at a level that is affordable and equitable. Although the future generation inevitably may have to carry part of the huge liability, the current generation must do its share of alleviating the burden.

To what level then should the contribution rate be increased? The current amount of CPP retirement pension for an average person is approximately $8,600. The simulation results (Table 3)

Table 2:   *Projected Average
Income and YMPE, 1995–2044*

Age	Year	Income	YMPE
		(constant 1995 $)	
21	1995	11,764	34,900
22	1996	14,445	35,149
23	1997	16,581	35,507
24	1998	18,737	35,863
25	1999	20,914	36,201
26	2000	23,111	36,596
27	2001	25,328	36,934
28	2002	26,714	37,291
29	2003	28,125	37,664
30	2004	29,560	38,048
31	2005	31,021	38,440
32	2006	32,507	38,761
33	2007	33,601	39,159
34	2008	34,713	39,555
35	2009	35,844	39,945
36	2010	36,993	40,328
37	2011	38,161	40,702
38	2012	39,142	41,124
39	2013	40,138	41,471
40	2014	41,150	41,915
41	2015	42,178	42,282
42	2016	43,221	42,733
43	2017	43,997	43,105
44	2018	44,784	43,549
45	2019	45,581	43,961

Table 2 - continued

Age	Year	Income	YMPE
		(constant 1995 $)	
46	2020	46,390	44,386
47	2021	47,211	44,821
48	2022	47,525	45,260
49	2023	47,841	45,700
50	2024	48,159	46,138
51	2025	48,479	46,571
52	2026	48,800	47,033
53	2027	48,318	47,482
54	2028	47,821	47,951
55	2029	47,310	48,400
56	2030	46,785	48,894
57	2031	46,246	49,361
58	2032	46,102	49,831
59	2033	45,952	50,329
60	2034	43,374	50,792
61	2035	44,726	51,303
62	2036	45,457	51,800
63	2037	45,124	52,280
64	2038	44,695	52,791
65	2039	33,479	53,303
66	2040	32,641	53,811
67	2041	33,286	54,335
68	2042	32,430	54,868
69	2043	27,975	55,406
70	2044	23,431	55,925

Sources: Canada 1995a; 1995b.

Table 3:   *Varying Contribution Rates:*
Effects on the Actuarially Based Pension
and Accumulated Funds at Age 65

Annual Contribution Rate	Actuarially Based Annual Pension Amount[a]	Accumulated Funds at Age 65	Increase in Accumulated Funds
(percent)	*(1995 dollars)*		*(percent)*
4	4,861	82,686	
5	6,077	103,373	25.0
6	7,292	124,039	20.0
7	8,506	144,705	16.7
8	9,722	165,377	14.3
9	10,937	186,055	12.5
10	12,152	206,720	11.1
11	13,367	227,389	10.0

[a] Indicating the amounts of pension affordable according to their respective contribution rates.

Assumptions: 2 percent real rate of investment return; 40 years of contributions; retirement at age 65; life expectancy of 85 years.

indicate that a contribution rate of approximately 7 percent is the minimum required to finance actuarially this level of pension.

It is important to note that our simulation here, dealt only with retirement pensions, not disability or survivor benefits.[16] Continuing to provide these other benefits (a subject we deal with later) would require a contribution rate of 10 or 11 percent, according to other simulations we did but do not report here.

Also noteworthy is the way the simulation findings indicate that raising the contribution rate would lead to substantial

16 In 1971, these benefits accounted for more than half of the CPP's total expenditure. In recent years, the proportion has dropped to about a third. Participants in an "Experts Forum on Canada Pension Plan Reform," hosted by the Caledon Institute of Social Policy (May 1, 1996) anticipated, however, that liberal interpretation of disability rules would raise future expenditures in this area; we agree with this judgment.

increases in the funds accumulated (through contributions and investment) to the time of retirement. For example, going from 6 to 7 percent increases the accumulated funds by 16.7 percent.

Eliminating the YBE

Another apparently easy way to raise CPP revenues is to eliminate the year's basic exemption (YBE). Currently, contributions are made only on pensionable earnings above the exemption, but benefits are based on the full amount of pensionable earnings *including* the exemption. If the exemption were abolished, calculated contributions would be higher.

Adding the elimination of the YBE to our standard assumption, we ran a simulation (not shown here). It indicates that the accumulated funds would increase 12.53 percent if the YBE were eliminated.

This result supports eliminating the exemption. This option would, however, affect low-income people proportionally more than others. Moreover, many low-income people are part-time workers who rely on some level of welfare; eliminating the YBE would reduce their part-time income and might discourage them from seeking employment. The social and economic costs could be higher than the additional revenue.

Investing through the Capital Market

As already reported, historical evidence shows that investing through the capital market would provide the CPP with higher returns, over the long run, than it now gains from provincial securities (see Figures 5 and 6). To see the results, we ran a simulation varying the rate of investment return but otherwise holding our assumptions steady.[17]

---

17 Since the concern here was the accumulation of funds to the time of retirement rather than the disbursement of funds, the assumption about life expectancy was irrelevant. A longer life reduces the amount of pension payable but not the funds accumulated to retirement.

Table 4:   *Varying the Real Rate of Investment Return*

Increase in the Real Rate of Investment Return	Increase in Accumulated Funds at Age 65
	(percent)
From 1% to 2%	21.0
From 2% to 3%	22.1
From 3% to 4%	23.2
From 4% to 5%	24.3
From 5% to 6%	25.3
From 6% to 7%	26.2

Assumptions: 7 percent contribution rate; 40 years of contributions; retirement at age 65.

Table 4 reports the results: for every percentage point increase in real return, the accumulated funds increase by 20 percent or more. Notice that, because of the exponential nature of compounding, the increase grows faster and faster as the return rate goes up, providing impressive support for the idea of extending CPP investments into the capital market.

A much-used argument against this kind of suggestion is that investment by government-operated institutions is inefficient, is affected by political interference, and lacks accountability. The CPP currently has no independent authority to hold its investment activities accountable. Instead, it has a 16-member advisory board, appointed by the governor-general-in-council, whose responsibility is to "review the operation of the [Canada Pension Plan] Act, the state of the Canada Pension Plan Investment Fund, and the adequacy of coverage and benefits provided under the plan" (Canada 1990, 49). It is questionable whether such a board can be completely free of political interference.

Two Ontario government reports on public sector pension funds provide suggestions on how an independent authority could be established. The Rowan Task Force examined the management of funds such as the province's superannuation fund. Its report (Ontario 1988b) suggests that government frequently confuses its various roles in public sector pension plans, allowing political agendas to override the interest of contributors. And it recommends that plan members be provided with avenues for being involved in the decisionmaking process. A follow-up report (Ontario 1988a) strengthens the recommendations:

- Plan members are entitled to be involved in pension fund decision making.
- As a general principle, it would be preferable to have a pension fund board of governors, structurally distinct from employers and employees, but with representation from both groups. Such representatives would have fiduciary responsibility for the pension fund. (P. iii.)

The follow-up report also recommends that "pension funds [be invested] through the market" (ibid.), a direction that would not preclude investment in nonmarket government debt.

We believe these recommendations deserve serious consideration in the current pension reform debate.

Reducing Benefits

Benefit reduction, a different approach to strengthening the CPP's financial position, is inevitably controversial. Yet given the current and anticipated negative cash flows, it seems fiscally and socially responsible to consider this strategy. There are several options, some of them more palatable than others.

Lowering the Retirement Pension Directly

The most obvious way to reduce CPP expenditures is to reduce the size of retirement pensions. This strategy would make logical and fiscal sense since, as we have shown, the current retirement pensions are higher than their actuarial values (look back at Table 1).

Moreover, reducing retirement pensions might be justifiable because fewer retirees are considered to be living in poverty now. As recently as 1982, retirees headed 20.4 percent of families classified as living in poverty, but in 1992 the figure was only 8.0 percent; single mothers accounted for 31.6 percent in 1992, married couples with children another 31.6 percent, and married couples without children 13.8 percent (Finnie 1995). These statistics suggest that retirees are not necessarily the Canadians most in need.

Directly reducing benefits would, however, be politically difficult to implement and it might invite lawsuits (because the CPP has defined benefits).

Raising the Minimum Contribution Period

A different strategy for reducing pensions is to raise the minimum contributory period for full pension entitlement. The current rule is 10 years (120 months), but, as we have shown (see Table 1), even 30 years of contributions would be insufficient to finance the current level of benefits. The minimum contributory period should therefore be raised, with those not meeting the requirement being paid lower pensions.

This approach would be equitable, because income level is not directly related to the contributory period and individuals with a shorter contributory period are not necessarily the most in need. For example, a physician, who spends years in training, may have a shorter contributory period than an average worker, and given the limit on the amount of pensionable earnings, the former's annual contributions may not be significantly more than the latter's. Thus, over their working lives, the worker may contribute more than the physician, but the full pension for the two is the same. The current policy may thus benefit high-income professionals at the expense of average workers. If the pension benefit should, in principle, reflect contributions, it is justifiable to tie it to the contributory period (just as it is currently tied to the average earnings ratio).

Table 5:   *Contributory Period and Investment*
Return Required for Financing a CPP Pension

Contributory Period	Real Rate of Investment Return Required for Financing an $8,600[a] Annual Pension from Ages 65 to 85
(years)	*(percent)*
40	2.1
35	2.5
30	3.1
25	4.2
20	5.8
15	8.8
10	14.4

[a] In 1995 dollars.

Assumptions: 7 percent contribution rate; retirement at age 65; life expectancy of 85 years.

Using our standard assumptions, we ran several simulations to assess the contributory period required for the current level of retirement benefits ($8,600 a year). In one, we let the real rate of return vary. The results, in Table 5, show that 40 years of contributions are needed when the real rate of investment is 2.1 percent and that a short contributory period of 10 years requires a 14.4 percent return. Obviously, the latter rate is unrealistically high, but it confirms our belief that many past and some current pension recipients have received benefits higher than their contributions could support.[18] In brief, the findings present a strong case for increasing the length of the required contributory period.

Another simulation (Table 6) shows the financial effects of various contributory periods. A five-year reduction in the con-

18 As the plan matures, there are, of course, fewer and fewer benefit recipients with very short contributory periods.

Table 6:   *Varying the Contributory Period*

Change in Contributory Period	Reduction in Accumulated Funds at Age 65
(years)	*(percent)*
From 40 to 35	10.6
From 35 to 30	14.5
From 30 to 25	18.3
From 25 to 20	23.0

Assumptions: 7 percent contribution rate; 2 percent real rate of return; retirement at age 65.

tributory period reduces the funds accumulated at age 65 by at least 10 percent, and the reduction continues at an increasing rate. The results offer support for increasing the contributory period required for full pension entitlement; they also provide an indication of the appropriate proportions of benefit reduction for shorter contributory periods.

Eliminating the Dropout Provision

The current CPP formula allows 15 percent of low-earnings periods to be excluded from the pension calculation. This dropout provision raises the average earnings ratio and thus increases pension payments. Tests carried out on the similar QPP indicate that, if the dropout provision were eliminated, the contribution rate could be reduced by 0.5 percent in 2030 (Canadian Institute of Actuaries 1993). Our own simulation results (Table 7) reveal that eliminating the dropout provision would reduce the funds required for CPP pensions by 3 to 6 percent (depending on the length of the contributory period). Relative to other policy options, the effects of this one are not strong (although an approximately 5 percent saving on expenditure would still be significant). Moreover, policymakers should be careful about the dropout provision.

Table 7: *Eliminating the Dropout Provision*

Contributory Period	Reduction in Funds Required for CPP Pensions from Ages 65 to 85
(years)	*(percent)*
20	4.7
25	3.9
30	3.3
35	4.1
40	6.1

Assumptions: 7 percent contribution rate; 2 percent real rate of return; retirement at age 65, life expectancy of 85 years.

Without it, people who have contributed for long periods but had low-income years, such as unskilled female workers, would receive lower pensions than people with high incomes but short contribution periods, who may contribute less over time than unskilled workers.

Raising the Pensionable Age

Raising the pensionable age is a policy option that would both increase revenues by lengthening the contributory period and reduce expenditures by shortening the retirement period. Although the present trend is to retire before age 65 — the current average in Canada is about 62 — improvements in medical technology and changes in lifestyle are enabling people to have longer and healthier lives.[19]

Without changes, the CPP will have difficulty meeting pension payments as people live longer after retirement. With im-

---

19 In 1992, life expectancy for males was 72.1 years and 78.2 years for females. Projections indicate that, by 2100, life expectancy will increase to 80.3 years for males and 86.9 for females (Canada 1995b; Peron and Strohmenger 1994).

Table 8:   *Raising the Retirement Age*

Change in Retirement Age	Reduction in Funds Required for CPP Pensions as % of Accumulated Funds at Age 65	Increase in Accumulated Funds as % of Accumulated Funds at Age 65
	(percent)	
From 65 to 66	8.7	3.4
From 65 to 67	17.6	6.7
From 65 to 68	26.6	10.2
From 65 to 69	35.9	13.7
From 65 to 70	45.3	17.1

Assumptions: 7 percent contribution rate; 2 percent real rate of investment return; 40 years of contributions before age 65.

proved health, retired people are physically younger than they were in previous generations. It seems logical to raise the age for full pension entitlement perhaps to age 70 but allow for early retirement with actuarially adjusted pensions.

We simulated the results of delaying retirement until the age of 70 (Table 8). The accumulated funds would increase by 17.1 percent from five extra years of contributions and their corresponding investment returns; during the same period, an amount equaling 45.3 percent of the accumulated funds would be saved from pension payments that no longer had to be paid. By contrast, if retirement occurs at age 65, investment returns increase the accumulated funds by 10.4 percent over the next five years, but pension payments for the same period draw down the funds by 45.3 percent, resulting in a net decrease of 34.9 percent. In other words, by the time the contributor reaches age 70, the accumulated funds drop to 65.1 percent (100 percent − 34.9 percent) of the level at retirement. Postponing retirement by five years lets the accumulated funds increase to 117.1 percent of their level at age 65. The combined effects represent 79.9 percent (1.171/0.651) more funds in the balance by age 70.

The social costs of this option must, of course, be weighed against its benefits. Raising the pensionable age could reduce job opportunities for young people, especially if job growth is not adequate, and unskilled workers may have difficulty prolonging their careers. Moreover, since the trend today is to early retirement, pushing it later could provoke public resistance. By 2010, however, the baby boomers will have begun to retire, and there may be a labor shortage. People can be encouraged to stay on in their jobs for a few more years, particularly if the age of eligibility for regular retirement benefits is raised gradually over many years and if other public policy measures encourage older workers to remain in the labor force.

Taxing High-Income CPP Recipients

An additional tax on the CPP pension could be imposed on those who could most afford it. This alternative might be acceptable to some of the public because it would give the impression of being a tax that only the rich had to pay. Moreover, there are precedents for clawing back benefits from elderly high-income Canadians.[20]

Nevertheless, since CPP benefits have been "earned" through contributions and since they are already taxable, it is questionable whether they should be further taxed.

---

20 Since 1994, the age credit, which used to provide a 17 percent income tax credit to all seniors, has been subject to an income test, so it is now targeted to those with low or modest incomes. In 1989, legislation was passed to claw back the OAS pension from recipients with annual incomes of more than $50,000. As of July 1996, monthly OAS payments are being calculated and paid with the clawback amount subtracted (based on the prior year's tax return). Financially, this move yields a one-time savings of about $300 million for the public purse; symbolically, it represents the end of the universal character of the OAS (not all seniors now receive benefits in the first place). Also effective mid-1996, all OAS recipients who are nonresidents of Canada are being required to file a statement of their worldwide income to receive OAS benefits.

Eliminating Automatic Indexation

CPP pensions rise annually with increases in the CPI, so eliminating automatic indexation would have the effect of reducing retirement pensions through time. The Board of Trade of Metropolitan Toronto (1993) recommends replacing automatic indexation with a triennial review to determine the appropriate pension increase. Such a review could be done by the CPP's advisory board, the federal Department of Finance, or perhaps Statistics Canada.

This approach would be vastly unpopular among the current elderly population (and their adult children) because it would create financial difficulty, especially in times of high inflation, for those who rely heavily on the CPP. On the other hand, maintaining full automatic indexation may be financially defensible only if some of the other options canvassed here are adopted.

Maintaining the Current Purchasing Power

If the CPP pension increased only in relation to inflation, that increase would not raise the benefit's purchasing power. In the current formula, however, the calculation of the CPP pension is based on the YMPE, which often increases faster than inflation. Indeed, for the period after 1999, the CPP projects a 4.5 percent annual increase in earnings and a 3.5 percent inflation rate (Canada 1995b). If this forecast proves accurate, the YMPE will continue to rise above the inflation rate, leading to a higher level of purchasing power for the pension.

Expenditure rises could be reduced, however, by changing the formula for pension calculation to tie increases to inflation rather than the YMPE. Doing so would preserve automatic indexation but keep the pension at the current level of purchasing power.

We ran a simulation taking this approach. Using our other standard assumptions, we froze the YMPE for calculating pensions at its current level (with adjustment for inflation) but, in order not to affect contributions, we allowed the YMPE for calculating contributions to rise with projected increases in average earnings. The results (not shown separately here) indicate that such a change would result in an average saving of $97,165 per contributor, equaling 65 percent of accumulated funds.

Changing Survivor and Disability Benefits

Survivor and disability benefits now account for approximately a third of CPP payments,[21] a proportion never envisioned by the creators of the plan. Disability payments were added only in 1987. Survivor benefits were quite modest to begin with and were originally offered to widows who had been economically dependent on their husbands and had a continuing need for child care. Over the years, benefits were increased, extended to widowers and common-law spouses, and granted on the basis of age without regard to a need for child care. Today, given such social changes as the decrease in fertility, the growing economic autonomy of spouses, and the diversification of family forms, CPP survivor payments may be being made to a large number of people who do not need them.

Some commentators, such as the Canadian Institute of Actuaries (1993), propose reducing these benefits. We cannot, in good conscience, recommend giving less support to survivors or the disabled who need it, but we do question whether that support should be provided through the CPP, especially when current contributions are insufficient to support current retirement pensions.

The CPP is, in principle, a contributory pension plan. Survivor and disability benefits are not pension benefits but income transfer mechanisms. Thus, these benefits could be appropriately removed from the CPP and combined with the OAS, GIS, and benefits paid by workers' compensation boards (WCBs) to form a

---

21 It is estimated that, in 1996, survivor benefits will account for 13 percent of total CPP payments and disability benefits for 20 percent (Canada 1995b).

system that guarantees a sufficient level of income and is financed through general revenues.[22]

Recommendations

The debate on pension policy and reform needs to go beyond popular beliefs, which often focus on obvious single variables such as the graying of the Canadian population, and move toward an understanding of the complex interplay of factors influencing pension programs. We do not favor winding up and scrapping the CPP. It is not, in the light of the simulation results, inherently flawed, although some of its design features need prompt reform and the plan requires a sounder basis of financing.

The CPP has a continuing central role to play alongside the other parts of the retirement income system: the income-tested elderly benefits from government, tax-assisted savings, occupational pension plans, and private assets and investments. All contribute in various ways to the present wealth and future prosperity of the community. As a social policy institution, the CPP provides people with a portable foundation for other retirement vehicles, one that is linked closely with a multitude of private plans in the labor force but that offers virtual universality of coverage.

Public pension reform must take account of the distribution of social rights and resource obligations across generations and over time. In maintaining the sustainability of the CPP, policymakers must recall that it is a series of intergenerational relationships involving both the present balance between the pension benefits of the retired generation and the obligations of the working population and the future balance between the benefits that will go to the present working-age population and the con-

---

22 This recommendation points up what we see as some other unfinished business of social policy reform: the need to transform the existing patchwork of income support for people with various disabilities into a more effective and equitable *national* program.

tribution duties of the working generations through the twenty-first century. Any effort to reform the retirement income system must face these relationships.

Our analysis has drawn attention to two imbalances in the CPP's intergenerational contract: the low contribution rates over the system's first 20 years and the schedule of steady increases that will culminate in historically steep rates over the next three decades. We believe that policymakers should redress the CPP's unduly low contribution rate of the past and that the current generation should do something to alleviate the expected significant financial burden on future employees and employers.

Although our analysis indicates that current pension benefits are too high actuarially for the contributions received, we do not recommend a direct reduction in benefits for three reasons. First, a large proportion of current and near retirees (those, say, aged 55 and over) have planned their retirement expecting CPP benefits to continue at their current levels. Social security and equity suggest honoring these expectations. Second, such a reduction would be politically arduous to implement, if not practically unrealizable, because the CPP is a federalized social contract. Such intergovernmental agreements are both a valuable source of stability in an uncertain world and an impediment to quick and easy change. Social contracts exist as responses to key needs, and they are often the product of bitter disputes. Third, the simulation data strongly show that other policy reforms can transform the CPP into a financially sustainable program.

Seeking to honor past commitments and to acknowledge the rights of future generations, we call for the present generation to adopt new social duties and policy approaches. We recommend a fivefold package of reforms for putting the CPP on a financially sound basis today so that it will be socially and politically more acceptable tomorrow.

1. *Quickly raise the contribution rate, employee and employer combined, to 8 percent.* Increases in the contribution rate are

inevitable: the current rate is too low and cannot finance the current level of benefits. But the rate increases that the current CPP schedule calls for (Canada 1995b) start too low, end too high, and are spread over too long a period of time. Increasing the contribution rate sooner, rather than later, would save pain in the long run.

A 7 percent contribution rate would be sufficient to finance the current level of retirement benefits. According to present policy, however, retirement benefits will rise with earnings increases. In addition, the plan's unfunded liability grows monthly. An increase in the contribution rate to 7 percent alone will not solve the problem, however. We therefore recommend an 8 percent contribution rate. The additional percentage point would raise 14.28 percent more funds over the contributory period and, with other measures recommended here, pay off the existing unfunded liability.

2. *Invest contributions through the capital market.* For every percentage point increase in real return on investment, the accumulated CPP funds will increase by more than 20 percent (see Table 4). Historical evidence reveals that the capital market provides higher returns than public sector securities. Additional simulations point out that increasing the real rate of return from 1.5 percent (achieved by the CPP) to 3.5 percent (achieved by investment funds) would increase the accumulated funds by 49 percent. Investing through the capital market would, therefore, be a very effective strategy.

If the CPP is to invest through the capital market, an independent authority should be set up to regulate investment activities and to protect the interest of contributors.

3. *Gradually raise the retirement age for full pension entitlement to 70 years.* Raising the retirement age would increase revenues and reduce costs. For every year of delayed retirement, expenditures would be reduced by 3 to 5 percent and revenues would be increased by about 3 percent (see Table 8). Phasing in a rise to age 70, over, say, the next 20 or 25 years, would

have an overall effect of a 79.9 percent improvement in the fund balance. Since the current trend is to retire early, early retirement should be allowed, albeit with lower pensions.[23]

Altering the CPP retirement age would represent an alteration of the social meaning of retirement; the acceptability and effectiveness of this reform could be enhanced by complementary reforms dealing with occupational pension plans, early retirement incentive plans and employment-related initiatives for older workers. In addition, it would be important to ensure that the OAS and GIS (the new Seniors Benefit in 2001) and the SPA combined would provide adequate incomes for those who could not prolong their careers to meet basic needs.

4. *Freeze the retirement pension at its current level of purchasing power.* In light of the potential hardship to recipients, we do not advocate direct pension reduction, but in light of the CPP's financial difficulty, we recommend keeping the pension at its current level of purchasing power. In other words, the pension of the future would be based on today's YMPE with an inflation adjustment. The simulation indicates that this option would result in an average saving of 67 percent of the accumulated funds (including the return on the increased investment) over the retirement period.

5. *Remove survivor and disability benefits from the CPP and provide them under the WCB, OAS, and GIS.* Our first four recommendations would provide the CPP with enough funds to finance the retirement pension and gradually pay off the existing unfunded liability. These measures would not, however, be sufficient to support survivor and disability benefits. We recommend that those benefits be combined with those of the OAS and GIS and the WCBs to form a system that guarantees a sufficient level of income and that is financed

---

23 Our simulations do not include an early retirement provision, but the overall effect should not be great.

through general revenues. Taxes might have to rise, but the CPP would no longer be a hidden mechanism for financing income transfer programs.

Survivor and disability benefits currently account for about a third of the CPP's benefit expenditures, so this move would reduce those expenditures by the same proportion.

Individually, each of these policy options would make major improvements in the CPP fund balance. If they were implemented together, the interaction would make the effects even more dramatic.

We ran an additional simulation of the combined effects of our first four recommendations, comparing the results with the CPP's proposed rate increases (see Table 9).[24] The simulations indicate that, if CPP's proposed rate increases were implemented, instead of the options recommended here, the funds accumulated at age 65 would amount to $219,108, and if the pension amount were not fixed at the current level of purchasing power, it would grow to $12,599 at the time of retirement. Assuming a 1.5 percent real rate of investment return, the accumulated funds would drop to $171,129 by age 70. The recommended options would perform better. If the capital market could provide returns two percentage points higher than public sector securities (that is, up from 1.5 to 3.5 percent), the difference could be a 62 percent increase in fund balance. The recommended policy options should be able to provide enough funds to finance the CPP pensions with a surplus to absorb the existing unfunded liabilities.

Conclusion

By simulating the future of possible reforms to the CPP, we seek to stimulate informed policy discussions on the plan, whose

---

24 These simulations examined only the effects on the fund at the time of retirement, so we did not include the effects of removing survivor and disability benefits from the CPP.

Table 9: *Recommended Policy Options and the Proposed CPP Rate Increases*

Effects of Recommended Policy Options[a]

Real Rate of Return	Funds Accumulated at Age 70[b]
(percent)	*(1995 dollars)*
1.5	172,763
2.0	193,654
2.5	217,674
3.0	245,363
3.5	277,295

*Effects of Recommended Policy Options[a]
and of Proposed CPP Rate Increases*

Funds Accumulated at Age 70, Given:

Recommended Options and Market Rate of Return[b]	Proposed CPP Rate Increases plus 1.5% Real Rate of Return[c]	Difference
(1995 dollars)		*(percent)*
172,763	171,129	1.0
193,654	171,129	13.2
217,674	171,129	27.2
245,363	171,129	43.4
277,295	171,129	62.0

[a] Effects of removing survivor and disability benefits not included.

[b] Assumptions for recommended policy options: 45 years of contributions; retirement at age 70; life expectancy of 85 years; 8 percent contribution rate; benefits frozen at current level with inflation adjustments; investing through the capital market.

[c] Assumptions for the option based on proposed CPP rate increases: 40 years of contributions; retirement at age 65, life expectancy of 85 years; benefits grow with YMPE; 1.5 percent real rate of investment returns.

creation in the 1960s was a significant achievement of Canadian federalism and parliamentary government. Its restoration in the 1990s, as a national project, could help revive Canadians' collective sense of themselves in the pursuit of peace, order, and good government as well as dignity and security in old age.

Appendix

To set up the simulations described in the text, we had to project our average CPP contributor's annual income from 1995 to 2044 and YMPEs for those years (look back at Table 2). To do so, we used the following procedures.

1. Average income by age group was obtained from *Canada Pension Plan Contributors: 1993* (Canada 1995a). The data represent the current income distribution among CPP contributors divided into age groups of five-year intervals.

2. Incomes within each age group were estimated by straight-line averaging. For example, the average income for 20-to-24-year-olds is $13,881. We assumed this amount to be the income for the 22-year-olds, the median age within the group, and then adjusted it by year in equal proportion, forward and backward, to match income figures in adjacent age groups.

3. The income figures from step 2 were compounded using the rates of earning increase projected in the *Canada Pension Plan Fifteenth Actuarial Report* (Canada 1995b) for future years; those rates were assumed to be 4.5 percent after 1999.

4. The earnings-adjusted figures were then discounted back to their 1995 values using the inflation rates projected by the CPP (ibid.), which were assumed to be 3.5 percent after 1999.

The corresponding YMPEs for future years were compounded and discounted back using the same earning-increase and inflation rates mentioned in steps 3 and 4.

References

Board of Trade of Metropolitan Toronto. 1993. "Strategies for the Long Term Survival of the Canada Pension Plan." Letter to the Minister-designate of Human Resources and Labour.

Brown, R. 1993. "Canadian Retirement Income Social Security Programs Review and Prognosis." University of Waterloo, Waterloo, Ontario.

Canada. 1982. *Better Pensions for Canadians*. Ottawa: Supply and Services Canada.

————. 1990. Department of National Health and Welfare. *Report for the Year Ending March 31, 1989, Income Security Program*. Ottawa: Supply and Services Canada.

————. 1995a. Department of Human Resources Development. *Canada Pension Plan Contributors: 1993*. Ottawa: Supply and Services Canada.

————. 1995b. Office of the Superintendent of Financial Institutions. *Canada Pension Plan Fifteenth Actuarial Report*. Ottawa: Supply and Services Canada.

Canadian Institute of Actuaries. 1993. *Canadian Retirement Income Social Security Programs*. Ottawa.

Courchene, T.J. 1994. *Social Canada in the Millennium: Reform Imperatives and Restructuring Principles*. The Social Policy Challenge 4. Toronto: C.D. Howe Institute.

Doern, G.B., A.M. Maslove, and M.J. Prince. 1988. *Public Budgeting in Canada: Politics, Economics and Management*. Ottawa: Carleton University Press.

Federal, Provincial, and Territorial Governments of Canada. 1996. *An Information Paper for Consultations on the Canada Pension Plan*. Ottawa: Department of Finance.

Finnie, R. 1995. "The Economics of Divorce." In Martin D. Dooley et al., *Family Matters: New Policies for Divorce, Lone Mothers, and Child Poverty*. The Social Policy Challenge 8. Toronto. C.D. Howe Institute, 1995.

Hachette, D., and R. Luders. 1993. *Privatization in Chile: An Economic Appraisal*. San Francisco: International Center for Economic Growth.

James, E. 1995. "Averting the Old-Age Crisis." *Finance and Development*, June, pp. 4–7.

Lam, N. 1993. "Historical Analysis of Public Pension Schemes in Canada. In N. Lam, M.J. Prince, and J. Cutt, *Reforming the Public Pension System in Canada*. Victoria: University of Victoria, Centre for Public Sector Studies.

————, J. Cutt, and M.J. Prince. 1995. "Contain CPP Rate Increases." *Policy Options*, September, pp. 28–32.

————, J. Cutt, and M.J. Prince. 1996. "Reforming the Canada Pension Plan: Retrospect and Prospect." Paper presented at the School of Policy Studies, Queen's University, Kingston, Ont.

————, M.J. Prince, and J. Cutt. 1993. *Reforming the Public Pension System in Canada*. Victoria: University of Victoria, Centre for Public Sector Studies.

McDaniel, S.A. 1987. "Demographic Aging as a Guiding Paradigm in Canada's Welfare State." *Canadian Public Policy* 8 (3): 330–336.

Ontario. 1988a. Management Board of Cabinet. *Comments and Advice in Respect of the Rowan Report on the Investment of Public Sector Pension Funds*. Toronto: Queens Printer.

————. 1988b. *Task Force Report on the Investment of Public Sector Pension Funds*. Chair was Malcolm Rowan. Toronto: Queens Printer.

Moscovitch, A. 1993. "From the Conservative Ill-Fare State to a Renewed Welfare State." *Canadian Review of Social Policy* no. 32, pp. 1–12.

Peron, Y., and C. Strohmenger. *Demographic and Health Indicator: Presentation and Interpretation*. Statistics Canada, cat. 82-543. Ottawa.

Prince, M.J. 1996. "From Expanding Coverage to Heading for Cover: Shifts in the Politics and Policies of Canadian Pension Reform." In A. Joshi and E. Berger, eds., *Aging Workforce, Income Security, and Retirement: Policy and Practical Implications*. Hamilton, Ont.: McMaster University, Office of Gerontological Studies.

Robson, W.B.P. 1996. *Putting Some Gold in the Golden Years: Fixing the Canada Pension Plan*. C.D. Howe Institute Commentary 76. Toronto: C.D. Howe Institute. January.

Statistics Canada. Cat. 61-006. *Financial Institutions, Financial Statistics*. Ottawa.

World Bank. 1996. *Averting the Old Age Crisis: Policies to Protect and Promote Growth*. Oxford; New York: Oxford University Press.

Six Common Misperceptions about the Canada Pension Plan

Paul Dickinson

This paper is not a defense of the status quo, nor does it argue for or against any specific changes to the seniors' benefit system in general or to the Canada/Quebec Pension Plan (CPP/QPP) in particular. Rather, the paper investigates some popular perceptions that could affect the public's assessment of whatever policy options might be proposed. Specifically, it explains why some views of the CPP/QPP that have been popularized in the press are misperceptions or exaggerations.

The analysis adopts the perspective of the individual contributor and pensioner, and ignores broader issues about possible effects of the CPP/QPP on job creation and economic growth. The broader issues require a macroeconomic and general equilibrium analysis, which I do not undertake here. Because I do not purport to tell the whole story, I do not offer conclusions about what policies should or should not be adopted. Nor do I evaluate policy options, but I give perspective on the following popular misperceptions and exaggerations that could affect the evaluation process:

- Few of today's seniors are poor, and a large share of federal benefits goes to high-income seniors.
- The CPP[1] is regressive because workers with below-average income contribute a larger share of their earnings.
- The CPP does little to help low-income seniors.

---

1 Throughout this paper, I use data from the CPP. The QPP is designed like the CPP. Dollar amounts referred to in the text were current at time of writing.

- Future working generations will have less disposable income than today's workers, because CPP contribution rates must increase to finance the plan when the baby boomers retire.
- Today's younger workers will earn no interest on their CPP retirement contributions, and future generations will receive less in benefits than they pay in contributions.
- The CPP is approaching bankruptcy, imposing a second national debt on future generations, and creating unacceptably high transfers from generation X to the aging baby boom generation.

In addressing these misperceptions about the CPP, I do not ignore other programs such as Old Age Security and the Guaranteed Income Supplement (OAS/GIS) and income taxes. They too are part of the public benefit system for Canada's senior citizens and interact closely with the CPP.

There are certainly pressing reasons for examining the current system of seniors' benefits and tax allowances. At a time when many Canadians believe that budget deficits need to be reduced without increasing taxes, there seems to be serious concern that the CPP will be radically reduced or become unaffordable when the baby boomers retire. The increases in CPP contribution rates projected for the next 30 to 50 years have popularized questions — often reflected in the media — about whether the plan will be viable in its current form. For example, Andrew Coyne (1994), writing in the *Globe and Mail*, stated that "the poorest pensioners get little or nothing from the CPP....On the other hand, [society] is subsidizing the incomes of the 30 percent of retirees who inhabit the upper half of the social register." The president of the mutual fund division of one of Canada's large banks was quoted as saying (in Dalglish 1992): "The system is bankrupt. Nobody under 30 today will ever collect Old Age Security and CPP benefits unless they are destitute."

There is a real danger that such dramatic and unqualified predictions will be accepted without question, because the public knows little about the details of the CPP. One opinion poll found that only 59 percent of respondents could name the CPP/QPP without prompting (Gallup 1985). Once reminded, only 41 percent knew that contributions are related to earnings and 32 percent knew that CPP/QPP pensions are indexed to inflation. Only about 9 percent could make a reasonable estimate of the size of the pension. Statistics Canada concluded some years ago that the average Canadian either was not consciously planning retirement security or was "building on a foundation of ignorance" (Statistics Canada 1988).

There are valid reasons to examine some possible modifications to the public pension system, but extreme measures may become unavoidable if misperceptions are accepted as fact. If only a portion of the population withdraws its support because of misunderstandings, the attractive feature of a public plan's having a secure sponsor may be undermined. Other people have more reason to fear that the CPP's pension promise will not be kept. They too may withdraw their support from the CPP, even though they appreciate attributes such as compulsory contributions, portability, and fully indexed benefits.

If people expect CPP benefits to be radically reduced in the future, they will rightly view their past and present contributions as an unfair tax, not as an investment in their retirement income. Tax avoidance and evasion will become more acceptable because of feelings of injustice and inequity . This would further erode the tax base and make it even more difficult to deal with immediate fiscal problems. The possibility that the CPP's demise will become a self-fulfilling prophecy makes it even more important to examine the six common misperceptions. Before doing so, however, I describe the main features of the CPP and other federal programs affecting seniors.

The Federal Benefits System for Seniors

The main federal benefits for seniors are the contributory CPP; the noncontributory OAS, GIS, and the Spousal Pension Allowance (SPA); and income tax allowances.

The Canada Pension Plan

The CPP (and its counterpart, the QPP) was introduced in 1966 to provide a minimum earnings-related retirement pension. The plan was phased in over ten years, so that someone who started contributing in 1966 and retired in 1977, at age 65, would receive the full pension. Virtually all working people in Canada between ages 18 and 70 must contribute to the plan if annual earnings are above a minimum. Attractive features of the plan include universal coverage, full portability, immediate vesting, benefits fully indexed to inflation, low administrative costs, and, at least until recent perceptions took hold, a secure plan sponsor.

Contributions are compulsory, and split equally between employer and employee. (Self-employed persons contribute both the employer and employee shares.) Contributions are a percentage (the CPP *contribution rate*) of contributory earnings. *Contributory earnings* are actual earnings up to the Year's Maximum Pensionable Earnings (YMPE), and above the Year's Basic Exemption (YBE). The YBE is 10 percent of the YMPE. (In 1995, for example, the YMPE was $34,900 and the YBE $3,400.[2]) The YMPE increases each year in line with the Industrial Aggregate, Statistics Canada's measure of average wages and salaries, and does not fall even if the Industrial Aggregate does.

Earners must contribute to the CPP in every year that their actual earnings exceed the YBE, from age 18 to the participant's death, retirement, or age 71 (the contributory period), whichever comes first. Earnings after age 70 or after the participant starts receiving a CPP retirement pension are not subject to contributions. *Pensionable earnings* in any year are the actual earnings of a contributor, up to the YMPE. The YBE applies only to contributory earnings, not to pensionable earnings.

---

2 The CPP's chief actuary estimated that the contribution rate projected for 2030 would be reduced by about two percentage points if the YBE were abolished (Canadian Institute of Actuaries 1993).

The initial retirement pension at age 65 (the CPP's normal retirement age) is 25 percent of average pensionable earnings over the whole contributory period, adjusted for increases in the YMPE to the time of retirement. Once the pension is being received, it is indexed yearly to inflation. In 1995, the maximum initial retirement pension at age 65 was $713.19 per month, or $8,558.28 per year.

A number of years can be dropped from the contributory period to determine average pensionable earnings if such drop-outs will increase the pension. The general dropout allows the years of lowest earnings to be ignored, to a maximum of 15 percent of the contributory period — that is, seven years for someone retiring at age 65. There are extra dropouts for periods of disability and childrearing, and for the years between ages 60 and 65 that the pensioner takes as early retirement. Early retirement can be taken from ages 60 to 64 and late retirement from ages 65 to 71. In either case, the normal retirement pension is actuarially adjusted by half a percentage point for each month between the actual retirement and the normal retirement age of 65.

The CPP also provides benefits to people who suffer a severe and prolonged disability while under age 65, provided they have contributed for at least five of the last ten years or two of the last three years before the disability occurs. The disability benefit has a flat-rate portion and an earnings-related portion. In 1995, the maximum disability benefit was $10,256.88 per year. The disability benefit ceases at age 65, when the retirement benefit begins, or, if earlier, at death or at recovery.

The surviving spouse of a contributor is eligible for a survivor benefit if the contributor had contributed for a minimum number of years. This spouse must be at least 35 years of age, or be disabled, or have dependent children. Again, there is a flat-rate component and an earnings-related component, and the actual amounts vary by age and circumstance. Surviving spouses over the age of 65 are eligible for a survivor benefit of 60 percent of the deceased spouse's pension, with some limits on the combined pension if the surviving spouse also receives a personal CPP retirement pension. There are some benefits for orphans and for the children of disability-benefit recipients, and in 1995 there was a lump-sum death benefit to a maximum of $3,490.

In 1994, of total CPP expenditures, retirement pensions accounted for 64 percent, disability benefits for 19 percent, survivor benefits for 14 percent, orphans' benefits plus death benefits for less than 2 percent, and administrative costs for just above 1 percent.

When contributions exceed annual expenditures, the difference is posted to the CPP account in the federal government's consolidated revenue fund. At the end of each quarter, the difference between the account and a three-month operating balance goes into the Investment Fund, which is lent to provinces at the federal government's long-term bond rate of interest, in proportion to the contributions made by residents of each province. The loans to provinces, plus accumulated interest, can be drawn on to pay benefits in years when contributions are less than expenditures. The account is small relative to the total liabilities of the plan: in 1994, it was $41 billion, or about two and a half times annual expenditures.

The federal and provincial governments agree on CPP contribution rates for 25-year periods (the current agreement runs from 1992 to 2016). Federal and provincial ministers of finance review the agreement every five years in light of updated projections of revenues and expenditures from the CPP's chief actuary. The projections take into account economic, demographic, and financial factors.

The chief actuary's *Fifteenth Actuarial Report* (Canada 1995) has two scenarios for future contribution rates. Scenario A keeps contribution rates as they are in the current agreement and projects that the CPP account will be exhausted by the end of 2015. (The *Fourteenth Actuarial Report* [Canada 1992a] had projected that the account in 2015 would be 165 percent of the CPP's annual expenditures in that year.) After 2016, the contribution rates in Scenario A increase both to pay projected benefits and to replenish the CPP account. The projected rates after 2016 allow the account to reach a target value of two years of expenditures shortly after 2050. Comparing the new and old projections, new contribution rates would be 12.62 percent in 2020 instead of 11.3 percent and 15.43 percent in 2030 instead of 13.04 percent.

The higher contribution rates would be caused by a projected increase in expenditures attributable to the effect of a recent unexpected increase in disability benefit claims. Comparing the new and old projections, total CPP expenditures in 2016 would rise from $63.1 billion to $69.5 billion, although expenditures on retirement benefits would *fall* from $46.8 billion to $45.8 billion. Disability benefits in 2016, on the other hand, would increase from $6.7 billion to $14.5 billion in the new projections.

In Scenario B, contribution rates increase as early as 1997 from their levels in the current agreement. By 2016, the account is projected to be 179 percent of annual expenditures, instead of being exhausted as in Scenario A. The contribution rate in that year is projected to be 11.8 percent instead of 10.1 percent as in Scenario A; in 2020, 12.6 percent instead of 12.62 percent; and in 2030, 13.91 percent instead of 15.43 percent . Contribution rates in Scenario B are higher than in Scenario A before 2020, lower between 2021 and the late 2050s, and about the same thereafter.

OAS, the GIS, and the SPA

Old Age Security is a noncontributory, flat-rate, taxable benefit payable to all eligible seniors aged 65 and over and is funded out of federal general tax revenues. The maximum OAS benefit in 1995 was $4,690.89. Eligible for this maximum amount are:

- people who were at least 25 years old on July 1, 1977; who were resident in Canada at that time (or who have had some prior residence in Canada since age 18); and who have lived in Canada for the ten years immediately prior to their applying for benefits; and

- people who were less than 25 years of age or who were not resident in Canada before July 1, 1977, but who have lived in Canada for at least 40 years after age 18.

Other people over age 64 are eligible for a partial benefit of one-fortieth of the maximum for each year they have lived in Canada after age 18, provided they have lived in this country for at least ten years or come from a country with which Canada has an international agreement (those who come from one of these countries need live in Canada for only one year to become eligible). The individual who turns 65 after one year in Canada is eligible for one-fortieth of the maximum OAS, and receipt of OAS makes him or her eligible for the GIS as well. The OAS is payable indefinitely to seniors living outside Canada, provided they have lived in Canada for at least 20 years since age 18. Otherwise, it is payable for six months following departure and is resumed when the pensioner again takes up residence in Canada.

Although the OAS nominally is a flat-rate benefit, it is in fact income tested by the tax system. The OAS repayment, popularly known as the OAS clawback, is 15 percent of income in excess of $53,215, to a maximum of the OAS benefit. The income level where the clawback starts is indexed to inflation less three percentage points. Currently, the maximum OAS benefit is fully repaid in extra taxes when total income reaches $84,195. The benefit cheque is sent out regardless of income, and in the National Accounts the repayment is treated as income tax revenue, not as a reduction in the cost of OAS.

The GIS is a nontaxable, income-tested benefit for low-income seniors aged 65 or more who receive OAS. In 1995, the GIS benefit was $10,265 for a single person and $16,643 for a couple, minus OAS benefits and half of other income. For a single person with no other income, the maximum GIS benefit is $5,574 on full OAS, and $10,148 on one-fortieth of the full OAS. For a senior couple, the maximum GIS is $7,261 if the couple has two maximum OAS benefits, and $16,408 if it has two OAS benefits of one-fortieth of the maximum. Some provinces give extra benefits to low-income seniors — for example, Ontario's Guaranteed Annual Income Supplement (GAINS-A) program is an income-tested benefit that is also reduced by one-half of other income.

The Spousal Pension Allowance (SPA) is an income-tested, nontaxable benefit payable to a senior's spouse aged 60 to 64. Essentially, the SPA gives low-income couples the same OAS/GIS income guarantee that they would have if both partners were over age 65.

Taxes and Tax Allowances

Basic federal tax (BFT) is 17 percent of taxable income up to $29,590, plus 26 percent on the next $29,590, plus 29 percent on the portion over $59,180, minus tax allowances. The turning points between tax brackets and the personal tax allowances are indexed to inflation less three percentage points. There is a federal surtax of 3 percent of BFT up to $12,500, and 5 percent of the portion of BFT above $12,500. Except for Quebec, which has its own tax rates and collects its own tax, provincial taxes are a percentage of BFT, with each province setting its own rate.

The personal tax allowances are transformed into tax credits, which are deducted from taxes instead of from taxable income. The basic allowance is 17 percent of $6,456 for the tax filer and $5,380 for a spouse filing jointly. With the 3 percent surcharge and a provincial tax rate of, say, 60 percent, the basic allowance of $6,456 reduces total taxes by $1,789 (163 percent of 17 percent of $6,456). The federal tax allowance on CPP contributions is 17 percent of the contribution. In 1994, the employee's share of contributions at YMPE was $640.76; the CPP allowance would therefore reduce combined federal and provincial tax by $177.55.

Two tax allowances benefit seniors in particular. The age allowance reduces BFT by 17 percent of $3,482. The private pension income allowance (which is not restricted to seniors) reduces BFT by 17 percent of $1,000. The age allowance falls by 15 percent of income in excess of $25,291. As with the OAS clawback, the income level at which the allowance starts to fall is indexed to inflation minus three percentage points. In 1995, a senior who was single paid no tax on GIS benefits nor on the first $10,938 of other income.[3] With the GIS benefit reduction and federal-provincial income taxes, a taxpaying GIS recipient can face a combined marginal tax rate between 70 and 80 percent, depending on the provincial tax rate.

Dealing with Misperceptions

The information just reviewed brings the CPP into clear focus *within* the whole system of seniors' benefits and allowances, providing the correct context in which to examine the six common misperceptions. I now deal with each of these in turn.

> ### Misperception 1: Few of today's seniors are poor, and a large share of federal benefits goes to high-income seniors.

Here, I examine three critical questions: How do seniors' benefit levels compare with so-called poverty lines? What proportion of seniors is below which poverty lines? What transfer payments go to seniors in different ranges of income? As well, I briefly discuss redistribution through the private pension system to help keep the public system in the proper perspective.

Benefit Levels and the Meaning of Poverty

Poverty is a relative concept. The issue is not the basic survival of seniors but whether they can afford a lifestyle Canadian society considers decent. Statistics Canada's Low-Income Cut-Offs (LICOs) are the most commonly used measures of this type of "relative adequacy".[4] As Table 1 shows, there are different LICOs for

---

3 This assumes the senior has at least $1,000 of private pension income.

4 Statistics Canada takes pains to refer to these benchmarks as "low-income lines," which is a less subjective term than "poverty lines."

Table 1:   *Statistics Canada's*
            Low-Income Cut-Offs in 1993

Region	Single Person		Couple	
	Before-Tax LICO	After-Tax LICO	Before-Tax LICO	After-Tax LICO
	(dollars)			
R1	16,482	13,611	20,603	16,609
R2	14,137	11,466	17,671	13,990
R3	14,039	11,289	17,549	13,774
R4	13,063	10,315	16,329	12,587
R5	11,390	8,924	14,348	10,889

Source: Data provided to the author by Statistics Canada.

singles and couples and for each of five regions classified according to population density. The highest LICO is for urban areas with more than half a million people (R1), and the lowest is for rural areas (R5). In 1991, almost 60 percent of single OAS recipients lived in the large urban areas.

One set of LICOs is used for before-tax income and another, much less commonly used set for after-tax income. In fact, however, using after-tax income is a better way to compare seniors with non-seniors. Since seniors have special tax allowances and GIS benefits are not taxable, after-tax income is a larger percentage of before-tax income for seniors than for non-seniors.

Take a single senior in 1991 whose only income was the maximum OAS/GIS benefit and the tax credit for the goods and services tax (GST). If the senior lived in an urban area, his or her before-tax income would have been $5,106 below the before-tax LICO but after-tax income would have been $2,832 below the after-tax LICO. If the senior lived in a rural area, even before-tax income would have been $1,750 *above* the before-tax LICO. Adding the maximum CPP pension would have reduced the GIS by half the CPP, which would have raised before-tax income to

$1,439 below the before-tax LICO in an urban area but put after-tax income $305 *above* the after-tax LICO. In fact, adding the maximum CPP pension would have put single seniors above the after-tax LICOs everywhere except in large urban areas. A senior couple would have fared even better: OAS/GIS benefits and the GST credit alone would have put them above the before-tax LICOs everywhere except in large urban areas. In those areas, before-tax income would have been $1,268 below the before-tax LICO, or only $634 per person.

The after-tax LICOs show that OAS/GIS levels are significantly more adequate than are indicated by the before-tax LICOs, especially for single seniors outside large urban areas, and for senior couples regardless of region. Indeed, the federal tax/benefit system ensures that no senior who retires on a CPP pension reasonably close to the maximum will be significantly below the after-tax LICOs, even in urban areas.

A "reasonable" standard of adequacy is largely a judgment call, and other benchmarks do exist. One set of before-tax poverty lines is considerably lower than even the after-tax LICOs (Sarlo 1992). For a single person in 1994, these lines ranged from a high of $7,805 in British Columbia to a low of $5,938 in Saskatchewan (Shillington, Ross, and Lochhead 1994). For a couple in these provinces, the lines ranged from $10,817 to $8,958. Only 1 percent of seniors have incomes below these benchmarks (Coyne 1994), which is not surprising since they are significantly lower than even the OAS/GIS benefit level for single seniors ($10,170 in 1994) and for senior couples ($16,490).

This alternative set of benchmarks is more a subsistence standard of adequacy than a reasonable relative standard. For example, a studio apartment in the student district of Montreal cost about $300 per month in 1994. Add $25 per month for basic telephone service — a necessity for seniors — and $15 per month for electricity. The 1994 benchmark for Quebec was $6,606 per year, or $550.50 per month, which left the single senior with roughly $7 per day for food, clothing, household goods, transportation and medical expenses, and entertainment. Even with provincial subsidies for transportation and accommodation, few Canadians would agree that $7 per day for all these expenses would be sufficient to lift a retired senior out of poverty.

The Incidence of Low Income

The incidence of low income is the proportion of people below whatever low-income benchmarks are used. In 1992, one in five seniors (18.6 percent) was below the LICOs, compared with one in six (16.1 percent) of the whole population. Some people (for example, Coyne 1994) have used these figures to argue that seniors, as a group, are no worse off than the rest of the population, but the picture changes when the definition of the group is changed.

By the late 1980s, the proportion of seniors below the LICOs was much lower than in the early 1980s. As Table 2 shows, however, there were substantial differences among subgroups. The proportion of single seniors below the before-tax LICOs actually fell from 65.2 percent in 1981 to 47 percent in 1989, but this left almost half of all single seniors below the before-tax LICOs. Indeed, in some categories, most single seniors were still below before-tax LICOs in that year: 52.2 percent of single female seniors, 54 percent of single seniors aged 75 and over, and 58 percent of single seniors in metropolitan areas.

The picture improves when after-tax LICOs are used. While almost half (47 percent) of single seniors were below the before-tax LICOs in 1989, only a quarter (25.4 percent) were below the after-tax LICOs. Also in 1989, the proportion of senior couples below the after-tax LICOs (3.3 percent) was less than one-third of the proportion below the before-tax LICOs (10.9 percent). Therefore, the incidence of low income among seniors was much less when using the after-tax LICOs than when using the before-tax LICOs, although it is the latter statistics that are normally reported.

Reflecting regional differences in the LICOs, single seniors living in big cities account for the vast majority of all seniors below

Table 2:   _The Incidence of Low Income
among Seniors, 1981 and 1989_

	Using Before-Tax LICOs		Using After-Tax LICOs	
	1981	**1989**	**1981**	**1989**
Singles	65.2	47.0	48.8	25.4
Male	55.8	31.6	37.9	17.0
Female	68.7	52.2	52.6	28.1
GIS recipients		67.1		34.7
Age 65–74	49.8	40.1	44.2	21.1
Age 75 +	70.8	53.7	53.7	29.6
Big city		58.0		44.6
Other		37.8		9.2
Couples	13.3	10.9	4.1	3.3
Big city		20.0		6.5
Other		4.2		0.8

Note: Figures are author's estimates based on data from Statistics Canada's Survey of Consumer Finances. The 1986-based LICOs have been adjusted for inflation to 1989, and (lower) 1978-based LICOs adjusted for inflation to 1981.

Source: Canada 1992b.

the after-tax LICOs. In 1989, nearly 45 percent of single seniors in big cities, but fewer than 10 percent outside big cities, were below the after-tax LICOs. For senior couples, fewer than 7 percent were below the after-tax LICOs in big cities, and practically none elsewhere. In fact, it is almost impossible for senior couples outside metropolitan areas to be below the after-tax LICOs unless they do not receive OAS or they receive it but do not apply for the GIS.

Benefits to High-Income Seniors

In 1992, the OAS and CPP paid $10 billion to households with incomes over $53,800 (Coyne 1994). It has been argued that these figures show perverse redistribution, because "all these cheques to the rich [are] subsidizing the incomes of the 30 percent of retirees who inhabit the upper half of the social register" (ibid.).

There is more to these numbers, however, than meets the eye. The amount of redistribution depends on *net* transfers between income groups, not on the gross dollars paid by one or two programs. In 1993, about 40 percent of CPP/QPP pensions were returned to the federal and provincial governments through lower GIS payments, lower expenditures on other federal programs, and higher federal and provincial income tax revenues. The CPP/QPP reduced the cost of the GIS alone by more than $3 billion, and reduced federal and provincial budget deficits by an estimated $5.76 billion — about 31 percent of CPP/QPP expenditures in fiscal year 1993/94 (Dickinson 1994).[5]

It has been argued that the CPP is regressive because contributions take a bigger share of the earnings of low-income workers than of higher-income workers, it does little to increase the income of the lowest-income seniors, and it pays benefits to high-income seniors. The first two arguments are addressed in later discussions of other misperceptions. The third argument, however, must be dismissed out of hand. The CPP is an earnings-replacement program in which each individual's benefits are related to his or her contributions. To complain that the CPP pays pensions to high-income retirees is like complaining that private pension plans pay bigger pensions to people who contribute more to them. It is only fair that people who pay more into their pension plans should get more out of them.

How regressive, in fact, are the noncontributory programs for seniors? In fiscal year 1993/94, the federal government paid out $19.8 billion in OAS/GIS and SPA, comprising $4.4 billion for GIS, $15 billion for OAS, and $0.4 billion for SPA (Canada 1994). More than 40 percent of the total went to GIS recipients. The age

---

5 These numbers were simulated using the Department of Human Resources Development's SIMulation-TABulation model (SIMTAB). Estimates do not include the effect of CPP/QPP contributions on business tax revenues, or on provincial programs for seniors.

tax credit cost the government another $1.5 billion, plus $0.3 billion for the tax credit on private pension income, for a total gross cost of $21.6 billion. However, $2.2 billion was recovered in extra federal taxes on OAS, comprising $0.4 billion from the clawback and $1.8 billion from taxes on benefits not clawed back. Therefore, the net federal cost was about $19.5 billion — some $300 million *less* than the gross cost of OAS/GIS/SPA alone. More than one-third of net federal benefits and allowances went to households with total incomes below $15,000, and one-half went to households with total incomes less than $20,000. Almost two-thirds of net federal benefits and allowances went to the 60 percent of seniors households with incomes less than $25,000, and about one-quarter went to the 30 percent of households with more than $30,000. Less than 10 percent went to the one in eight seniors households with incomes above $50,000.

At first glance, these numbers suggest that the per capita share of net federal benefits going to seniors is fairly even across income ranges. However, this interpretation overlooks three important points. First, the data refer to households with seniors, not to seniors *per se*. Second, the income ranges refer to the income of the household, not to the income of seniors in the household. Third, household income *includes* OAS, GIS, and SPA benefits.

On the first point, the statistics on the incidence of low income suggest that most (likely the large majority) of the higher-income seniors households consist of senior couples. Therefore, the two-thirds of net federal benefits and allowances going to the 60 percent of seniors' *households* with incomes below $25,000 would, in fact, be going to less than 60 percent of *seniors*. Also, the 10 percent of benefits and allowances going to the one in eight households with incomes above $50,000 would actually be going to more than one in eight seniors.

The second point highlights the fact that some seniors are in higher-income households because such households have younger members who are working, not because the seniors have high incomes.

The third point shows that some seniors would not be in the higher income ranges if they did not receive benefits. A senior couple with two maximum OAS benefits and a total income of $25,500 would have only about $16,500 without OAS. Indeed, it has been estimated that three-quarters of unattached seniors would be below the before-tax LICOs were it not for OAS/GIS benefits and CPP/QPP pensions (Chawla 1991).[6] Also, the difference between the incidence of low income among single seniors using before-tax LICOs (47 percent) and that using after-tax LICOs (25.4 percent) shows that 21.6 percent of single seniors are not very far above the after-tax LICOs, even with OAS/GIS and CPP benefits.

Therefore, public benefits lift many single seniors above the gross LICOs, but not very far above. An extra tax dollar transferred to someone $5 above the line is better targeted and less regressive than an extra tax dollar transferred to someone $50,000 above the line. Many more seniors would be below the low-income lines were it not for OAS/GIS benefits.

Even so, OAS and special tax allowances do increase the level of income below which seniors are net recipients of the tax/transfer system (excluding CPP). For a senior couple, income taxes are less than two maximum OAS payments until total income is about $40,000, after which the couple pays more income taxes than it receives in benefits. A single senior is a net recipient until income is almost $25,000. These breakeven levels are higher than the levels for nonseniors who have no children to support. Whether the difference is too high *in principle* is a societal judgment about the standard of living that Canada's retired seniors should enjoy relative to others. It is one thing to argue that *practical* constraints, such as interest on the national debt, might make the difference too costly. It is quite another thing to argue that any regressivity is undesirable in principle.

---

6 Chawla's estimates use the (inflation-adjusted) 1978-based gross income LICOs, which are lower than the 1986-based LICOs used in Table 2.

In sum, the OAS and tax allowances do redistribute some-what to high-income seniors, but the number of such people and the amount transferred to them cannot be inferred from the evidence presented. Perverse redistribution to high-income sen-iors is exaggerated by looking at the gross cost of seniors' benefits instead of the net cost, by looking at household income instead of seniors' income, and by treating pensions from the contributory CPP like noncontributory benefits paid from (progressive) income tax revenues.

Private Pensions

To conclude this discussion about regressivity and perverse redis-tribution, some observations are necessary about the redistribu-tive effects of private Registered Pension Plans (RPPs) and Registered Retirement Savings Plans (RRSPs). This will help to put the public plan into proper perspective.

The income tax system defers taxes on contributions to pension plans, and on the interest that accrues in the plans, from the time contributions are made until the time the benefits are received. Deferred taxes are essentially an interest-free loan from the government. Since contributions to RPPs and RRSPs are deducted from taxable income, people in higher tax brackets get a bigger interest-free loan per dollar contributed than people in lower brackets. Also, people in higher brackets contribute many more dollars to private plans than people in lower brackets.

If provincial taxes are, say, 58 percent of basic federal tax, the loan per dollar contributed to the CPP is approximately 27 cents in all tax brackets,[7] because the tax allowance is given as a tax credit rather than as a deduction from taxable income. The loan per dollar contributed to a private plan is 27 cents in

---

7 That is, 161 percent of 17 percent with the 3 percent federal surcharge and 58 percent provincial tax. In fact, the loan rises to almost 28 cents on the dollar at higher incomes, where the surcharge is 5 percent.

the 17 percent federal tax bracket, but 42 cents in the 26 percent bracket and more than 46 cents in the 29 percent bracket. For people in higher brackets, the CPP's harsher treatment reduces the after-tax rate of return on contributions to the public plan.

The CPP replaces 25 percent of pensionable earnings while the norm for employer-sponsored RPPs is 70 percent, and pensionable earnings can go much higher than the CPP's maximum pensionable earnings. In 1989, only 39 percent of workers in the private sector aged 20 to 64 were in employer-sponsored pension plans (Frenken and Maser 1992). Coverage was especially poor for low-income workers and workers in small firms. More than 80 percent of workers earning between $40,000 and $60,000 were covered, but only 27 percent of workers earning less than $20,000. Seventy-two percent of workers in firms employing more than 500 people were covered, but less than 15 percent in firms employing fewer than 20 people. About one in three covered workers was in a plan with a pension partially indexed to inflation, and only about one in eight was in a plan with full protection against inflation (Weitz 1992).

In fact, RPP coverage has *declined* in the past few years, and there is little prospect of a significant increase in the near future. Many new jobs created in recent years have been low wage and in the services sector, and many are also short term or part time jobs (Economic Council of Canada 1990). For example, between 1981 and 1991, part-time workers increased from 9 percent to 19 percent of all workers (Frenken and Maser 1992). Such jobs are less likely to have employer-sponsored pension plans.

RRSPs, on the other hand, have become the growth vehicle for private pensions. Again, however, the participation rate among low-income workers is quite small. In 1987, little more than 1 percent of RRSP contributions came from the 34 percent of tax filers with incomes below $10,000 (Frenken 1990). In 1992, only one-quarter of people earning less than $30,000 contributed to an RRSP, and their average contribution was less than $2,000 (Ingerman and Rowley 1993).

In sum, more higher-income workers contribute to RPPs and RRSPs than do lower-income people, their contributions per person are higher, and the interest-free loan they receive, in the form of deferred taxes, per dollar contributed is bigger. Even if the perversely redistributive effects of the tax treatment are acceptable because RRSPs encourage national savings and economic growth — a presumption called into question by Christopher Ragan elsewhere in this volume — a proper perspective on the public pension plan should at least recognize the difference between the tax treatment of private pension plans and the public plan.

Misperception 2: The CPP is regressive because workers with below-average incomes contribute a larger share of earnings.

The previous section looked primarily at the redistributive effects of benefits and tax allowances. This section addresses the perception that CPP contribution rates are regressive because workers with below-average incomes contribute a larger share of their earnings than do other workers. Since I focus on perceptions, I do not enter into the debate about whether, or by how much, the employers' share of CPP contributions affects employment and wage rates.

Contributory earnings at the Year's Maximum Pensionable Earnings (YMPE) are 90 percent of total earnings, which means that contributions are the contribution rate multiplied by 90 percent of earnings. At all other levels of earnings, contributions are the contribution rate multiplied by less than 90 percent of earnings. The bigger the difference between earnings and the YMPE, plus or minus, the smaller the share of earnings that is contributed to the CPP. Below the YMPE, contributory earnings are less than 90 percent because the Year's Basic Exemption (YBE) is more than 10 percent of actual earnings. Above the YMPE, contributory earnings are less than 90 percent of actual earnings because the CPP does not cover the portion of earnings above the YMPE.

Table 3 shows that the share of earnings contributed by the worker who is at YMPE is one-eighth more than the share contributed by the worker who earns half the YMPE,[8] simply because the share of earnings on which contributions are payable at YMPE (90 percent) is one-eighth more than the share at half the YMPE (80 percent). But the YBE does not apply to pensionable earnings, so both workers get a pension of 25 percent of actual earnings even though the lower-income worker contributes a smaller share of earnings.

The CPP is therefore *progressive* on earnings up to the YMPE. Pensions are not proportional to contributions, as some people argue they ought to be, and they certainly are not regressive. The share of total earnings contributed is less above the YMPE than at it, but this is not regressive either. Forcing people to pay pension contributions on earnings that are not pensionable would not be progressive or even proportional — it would simply be unjust.

Public reports about future CPP contribution rates often gloss over the details of the plan or fail to spell out their ramifications. These commentaries leave the impression that the CPP will take between 6 and 7 percent of every employee's earnings in 2030 (or even more than 13 percent if the reader does not recognize that the employer pays half). Clearly, this is not the case, partly because of the difference between earnings and contributory earnings, and partly because of the tax credit on contributions. For example, as column 6 of Table 3 shows, the employee's net contribution in 2030, after allowing for the CPP tax credit, is projected to be 4.55 percent of earnings at YMPE, 4.04 percent at half the YMPE, and 2.27 percent at twice the YMPE.[9]

---

8 Self-employed contributions are twice the shares in Table 3. Employer contributions equal employee contributions, but the employer's after-tax contribution depends on business or corporate tax rates.

9 These contribution rates are those of Scenario B, and provincial taxes are 58 percent of basic federal tax.

Table 3:   *Employee Contributions as a Share of Earnings,*
             1995 and 2030, using Scenario B Contribution Rates

Earnings as % of YMPE (1)	Contributory Earnings as % of Earnings (2)	1995 Contributions		2030 Contributions	
		Before Credit (3)	After Credit (4)	Before Credit (5)	After Credit (6)
		(percent)			
20	50	1.35	0.98	3.48	2.53
50	80	2.16	1.57	5.56	4.04
60	83	2.25	1.63	5.80	4.21
100	90	2.43	1.76	6.26	4.55
150	60	1.62	1.18	4.17	3.03
180	50	1.35	0.98	3.48	2.53
200	45	1.22	0.88	3.13	2.27

Note: Taxes are 161 percent of basic federal tax (BFT), with provincial taxes at 58 percent
        of BFT and the federal surcharge at 3 percent of BFT. The CPP employer-plus-
        employee contribution rate is 5.4 percent in 1995 and 13.91 percent in 2030, as in
        the chief actuary's Scenario B (Canada 1995).

Nor does the 13.91 percent contribution rate projected for 2030 mean that employers will pay 6.96 percent of their payroll to the CPP. The employer's contribution will be 6.26 percent of payroll if, and only if, all employees earn exactly the YMPE. But if one-third of employees are at each of 20 percent, 100 percent, and 180 percent of YMPE, contributory earnings will be 63 percent, and the employer's CPP contributions will be 4.4 percent, of payroll. If the payroll were, say, 60 percent of production costs, CPP contributions would be 2.6 percent of production costs.

Misinterpreting by how much today's CPP contributions actually reduce an employee's net income re-inforce the misperception of an increasingly regressive program in the future. If only 41 percent of Canadians recognize that CPP contributions are related to earnings (Canada 1989), how many realize that, for the vast majority of workers, a 13.91 percent contribution rate in 2030 will cost them between 2 and 4.5 percent of their earnings?

Misperception 3: The CPP does little to help low-income seniors.

The CPP has been called an "upside-down welfare program" because it pays higher benefits to people who need them least, and because the income-tested safety net confiscates the CPP pensions of low-income seniors. In Ontario, the combined benefit reduction rates of the federal GIS and the provincial supplement for low-income seniors (GAINS-A) is 100 percent. A senior whose only income other than OAS/GIS and GAINS-A is one-half the maximum CPP pension will have virtually the same total income as someone with no CPP at all. Consequently, the argument goes, forcing low-income earners to contribute to a program from which they get little or no benefit is highly inequitable, even bordering on the immoral (Courchene 1994).

In fact, it is this reasoning, not the program, that is "upside-down." First, there is nothing wrong with people getting a bigger pension if they contribute more. That is the point of earnings replacement. Second, while it is true that some of the lowest-income seniors in Ontario get 50 cents less GIS and 50 cents less GAINS-A benefit per dollar of CPP pension, this is not immoral. The combination of the GIS and GAINS-A can never leave CPP recipients with less income in retirement than they would have without the CPP pension, and it reduces the risk that low-income workers will have inadequate incomes when they do retire. Benefits such as the GIS and GAINS-A are paid precisely because other income, including the CPP, is very low. The false reasoning ignores inevitable tradeoffs between equally moral criteria, and reverses the roles of different parts of the seniors' benefit system.

Tradeoffs among Moral Criteria

A system with an income-tested safety net cannot avoid making tradeoffs among criteria of equity, adequacy, target efficiency, and program cost.[10] Equity and adequacy are both moral objectives, and meeting one at the expense of the other does not create an immoral system. It is a matter of priorities.

No doubt, the low-income senior with a CPP pension would be more than happy if the income-tested safety net did not treat the pension as income. Perhaps the equity criterion does argue that those who saved for retirement should get some benefit from their savings. But if income-tested programs such as the GIS and GAINS-A reduce their benefit-reduction rates, taxpayers will pay more money for more income-tested benefits to more seniors. In today's fiscal climate, increasing costs in this manner likely would be unacceptable. An alternative would be to keep costs constant by lowering both the benefit reduction rate and the maximum benefit, but improving equity at the expense of adequacy does not make a more moral system.

Perhaps the best way to judge the morality of the system is to ask the people who supposedly are treated inequitably and immorally: Would GIS/GAINS-A recipients prefer to receive a higher return on CPP but a lower disposable income? Would low-wage workers with unstable employment prefer to get a better return on CPP contributions and an increase in disposable income in retirement if they do not lose their jobs, but at a bigger risk of having less retirement income if they do lose their jobs? The reader can speculate on the answers.

Role Reversal

The role of contributory pensions is to replace earnings and reduce the *change* in living standards when someone moves from work to retirement. The role of an income-tested safety net is to ensure that the *level* of the senior's standard of living is acceptable to society. The safety net acts as a payer of last resort, the

---

10 A program is target efficient if a high proportion of benefits goes to the target population. If the objective is an "adequate" income, low target efficiency means that a high proportion of benefits go to people with more-than-adequate incomes.

last-payer program, to supplement income from private plans and from *first-payer* programs such as the CPP.

The CPP is a first-payer public program because it is earnings related and funded from contributions, with a defined relationship between contributions and benefits. It is not an income-tested, last-resort safety net funded from general revenues as is the GIS. The first-payer value of the CPP is the amount it would add to disposable income if there were no benefits or tax allowances specific to both seniors and nonseniors. The last-payer value of the CPP is the amount it actually adds to disposable income when all benefits and tax allowances are taken into account, including the age credit and OAS/GIS benefits available only to seniors. In effect, the last-payer value of the CPP is its net cost to the government.

The system as a whole cannot be evaluated using the last-payer values of each and every component since this would ignore the roles of different components. Moreover, the sum of all last-payer values need not equal the cost of the entire system. For example, for a single senior eligible for maximum OAS/GIS benefits in 1995, the last-payer values are $5,573 for the GIS and $0 for OAS,[11] yet OAS/GIS combined is $10,264!

Only by summing the *incremental* values as each component is added to the system *in sequence* will the sum of the parts necessarily equal the whole. The cost of the seniors' system equals the first-payer value of the CPP as I have defined it, plus the incremental cost of the seniors' tax allowances, plus the incremental cost of OAS/GIS. It makes sense to add the components in an order that is consistent with their different roles — the earnings replacement component first and the safety net component last. Upside-down reasoning reverses this order, putting the GIS first and the CPP last.

Table 4 shows first-payer and last-payer values of the maximum CPP pension in 1993 ($8,008), and half the maximum CPP pension ($4,004). Taxes are 58 percent of basic federal tax, and

---

[11] Because the GIS benefit is reduced by the full amount of the OAS benefit.

Table 4: *First-Payer and Last-Payer Values of the Maximum ($8,008) and Half the Maximum ($4,004) CPP Pension in 1993*

Income Range (1)	Private Pension (2)	CPP (3)	Share of CPP Added to Net Income		Value of CPP as % of Net Income	
			First Payer (4)	Last Payer (5)	First Payer (6)	Last Payer (7)
	($)		(%)	(%)	(%)	(%)
GIS, no tax	1,000	Half	100.0	50.5	31.2	15.7
GIS and tax	4,000	Half	90.2	36.7	26.0	11.2
		Full	82.3	37.5	42.8	19.5
Age-credit reduction	21,000	Half	72.6	64.1	11.9	10.5
		Full	63.8	57.9	19.3	17.5
OAS repayment	56,000	Half	58.1	49.0	5.3	4.5
		Full	54.9	45.0	9.7	7.9

Note: The first-payer value of the CPP is the CPP adjusted for induced changes in total taxes (158 percent of basic federal tax) and the GST credit; the last-payer value is the CPP adjusted for changes in all taxes and benefits, including GIS, age and private pension allowances, and the OAS repayment.

the only sources of income are private pensions, the GST tax credit, CPP pensions, and OAS/GIS. With only $1,000 of private pension income and no OAS/GIS benefits or special tax allowances, the first-payer value of CPP is its full amount because adding half the maximum CPP to the private pension does not move total income into the taxable range (column 4). With OAS/GIS and seniors' tax allowances in the system, adding CPP pensions reduces GIS benefits by half the CPP pension, and no taxes are payable.[12] The cost of the GIS is reduced by half the CPP pension (column 4 minus column 5), and the last-payer value of the CPP increases disposable income by half the CPP pension

---

12 I ignore the GAINS-A program because it is specific to Ontario.

(column 5). The first-payer value of the CPP is nearly one-third of disposable income (column 6), but the last-payer value is less than one-seventh (column 7).

With private pension income of $4,000, disposable income increases by 90 percent of half the maximum CPP at the first-payer value,[13] and by 82 percent of the maximum CPP. At the last-payer values, however, disposable income increases by little more than one-third of CPP pensions (36.7 percent and 37.5 percent). The GIS benefit is reduced by half the CPP, and most of the CPP pension is taxed at nearly 27 percent. Therefore, the combined effective tax rate on most of the CPP benefit is about 77 percent, higher than in any other income range.

First-payer and last-payer values differ by province. In Ontario's GAINS-A range, the first-payer value of half the maximum CPP is its full amount, but the last-payer value is close to zero. For the taxpaying GIS recipient in Newfoundland, the last-payer value is about 20 cents per dollar of CPP benefits because Newfoundland has a high provincial tax rate. Is this also immoral, or is the dividing line between morality and immorality somewhere between 20 cents and nothing?

To repeat, the CPP is an "upside-down welfare program" only if the system is turned upside down by reversing the logical sequence of the contributory earnings-related pension and the income-tested safety net. Reversing the sequence in this manner is inconsistent with the different roles of the different components of the seniors' system.

Misperception 4: Future working generations will have less disposable income than today's workers because CPP contribution rates must increase to finance the plan when the baby boomers retire.

There are two interpretations of the future affordability of the CPP. One is that contribution rates will increase the tax burden

---

13 That is, income taxes would be about 10 percent of the CPP's $4,004 pension if there were no age allowance or private pension allowance.

on future workers to the point where they will be *unwilling* to pay higher rates. The other is that higher CPP contributions will reduce disposable income to the point where future workers will be *unable* to pay higher rates.

Media reports tend to focus on higher dependency ratios when the baby boomers retires, higher CPP contribution rates, and the size of the increase in contributions. Since such reports ignore economic growth and growth in real earnings, they leave the impression that higher contribution rates will reduce the standard of living of future contributors below that enjoyed by current contributors. This raises the specter of a reduced ability to pay by people who are unwilling to "subsidize the retirement of a generation that will be better off than they are" ("Will we still feed them, when they're 64?" *Globe and Mail* [Toronto], Editorial, November 15, 1993). This interpretation, however, is not consistent with the very projections that raised the concerns.

Dependency Ratios

The broadest *dependency ratio* is the number of people of non-working age for each person of working age.[14] Currently, this ratio is lower in Canada than in other industrialized countries, and lower than it was in earlier years. In 1987, for every 100 people aged 15 to 64, there were 47 below age 15 or above age 64, down from 70 per 100 in 1965 (Chawla 1991). After 2010, however, the ratio is expected to climb rapidly, reaching 67 per 100 by 2030. Although Canada's ratio in 2030 is expected to be similar to the projected ratios in other Group-of-Seven (G-7) countries, Canada will have had to adjust to a bigger increase.

The composition of the ratio will also change. In 1980, the proportion of seniors in the Canadian population (10 percent) was lower than the average of other member countries of the Organ-

---

14 Obviously, the number of nonworking old and young people as a percentage of the working age population is higher than that number as a percentage of the total population, which is how the dependency ratio is usually reported.

isation for Economic Co-operation and Development (OECD) (12 percent), but the proportion in 2050 (21 percent) will be about equal to the projected OECD average (Gauthier 1991). The public sector cost of a senior has been estimated at about three times the cost of a young person, but this may change in the future. The cost of medical and attendant care may increase the net cost per senior as longevity increases, while the growth of tax-sheltered retirement savings may reduce the net cost per senior. The GIS and OAS in the clawback range are income tested but not asset tested. Savings outside tax shelters are assets, but savings withdrawn from tax shelters are income. Even if the tax treatment of RPPs and RRSPs causes no change in total saving, the growth of such plans will redefine some of the resources of seniors, from assets to income. This redefinition alone should increase tax revenue per senior and reduce income-tested benefits per senior. Also, of course, there will be more seniors.

Dependency ratios based solely on age do not show changes in the proportion of the population employed or in the labor force. Of the G-7 countries in 1987, Canada and Japan had the smallest number of seniors and youngsters for each member of the labor force (Chawla 1991). If participation rates of Canadian women grow to equal those of their male counterparts by 2021, this labor-force-adjusted dependency ratio may be the same then as now. If women's participation rates stay at 1986 levels, future labor-force-adjusted dependency ratios may still be less than in the 1950s and 1960s (Fellegi 1989).

Even if there were no baby boom, lower mortality rates and increased longevity would have increased seniors' dependency ratios and CPP contribution rates (see Misperception 6). The official projections of CPP contribution rates assume that, between 1986 and 2100, life expectancy at age 65 will increase by 30 percent (4.4 years) for men and 28 percent (5.4 years) for women (Canada 1992). Regardless of other demographic trends, future workers must contribute more if they wish to take their increased longevity as extra years in retirement.

Real Disposable Income

Official projections of CPP contribution rates assume an increase of real average earnings by 1 percent per annum.[15] This approximates the average annual growth in earnings per worker over the past 25 years (1.02 percent per annum). As explained earlier, the chief actuary has projected two sets of CPP contribution rates, Scenario A and Scenario B (Canada 1995). In Scenario A, the contribution rates to 2016 are as currently agreed between the federal and provincial governments, but the CPP account would be wiped out by 2015. In Scenario B, the contribution rates increase from the agreed levels as early as 1997. The contribution rate projected for 2030 is 15.43 percent under Scenario A and 13.91 percent under Scenario B. Both are higher than the previous projection of 31.04 percent (Canada 1992).

The increase in CPP contribution rates between the old and new projections is, however, solely due to the effect on projected expenditures of a recent and unexpected increase in disability benefit claims. In fact, when the new and old projections are compared, there is a rise in the share of contributory earnings required to pay all benefits in 2030, but the share needed only for retirement pensions remains unchanged (10.46 percent). The share needed for survivor benefits actually *falls* (from 1.4 percent to 1.34 percent), while the share for disability benefits more than doubles (from 0.95 percent to 2.06 percent).

The increase in disability claims may be a response to improved information about the CPP's disability benefits, but it may also be a response to economic forces such as unemployment. If it is the latter, and if the increase is not sustained, the latest projections may overestimate future contribution rates. In any case, the contribution rates of Scenario B are used in this section,

15 Average earnings are assumed to grow by 4.5 percent per year, with 3.5 percent annual inflation. To be exact, the real rate of growth is 0.97 percent per year.

with employer-plus-employee rates of 5.4 percent of contributory earnings in 1995, 12.6 percent in 2020, and 13.91 percent in 2030.

Table 5 shows that the percentage increase in real disposable income at YMPE (column 2) is minimal with income tax brackets and allowances indexed to inflation minus three percentage points, as they are currently. This is because the real value of income taxes paid by the average earner in 2020 is nearly double the real value in 1995. It seems highly improbable that income taxes on average earnings could increase from less than one-quarter (23.3 percent) of earnings in 1995 to more than one-third (34.2 percent) in 2020, and almost four-tenths (37.2 percent) by 2050.[16]

If earnings growth exceeds inflation, the share of earnings taken as income tax would increase even if tax brackets and allowances were fully indexed to inflation. Between 1995 and 2030, the real value of tax revenues would grow by 60 percent, and taxes plus CPP contributions at YMPE would take one-third of earnings in 2030 (column 5). However, even with this tax scenario, the employee's real disposable income would increase by one-quarter at YMPE, by about three-tenths at 150 percent of the YMPE, and by nearly one-third at 50 percent of the YMPE (the latter two are not shown in Table 5). The employee at YMPE is a worst-case situation, because contributory earnings are a higher proportion of total earnings than at any other level.

With tax brackets and allowances indexed to the growth in average earnings, real disposable income at YMPE increases by one-third between 1995 and 2030, and by one-half between 1995 and 2050 (not shown in Table 5). Real income tax revenues increase by almost one-third between 1995 and 2030, but the share of earnings taken in taxes falls by nearly one percentage

---

16 Two things should be noted about the tax scenarios. First, the projections keep the current marginal tax rates purely as a convenience. Only average rates are relevant for this analysis. Second, although the provincial rate of 54.5 percent of basic federal tax is low even by current standards, the composition of the total tax rate is less important than its level and rate of increase. The same combined rate of 57.5 percent of basic federal tax would be achieved if the federal surtax were removed and provinces were to raise their share by three percentage points.

Table 5: *Employee's Taxes and Real Disposable Income of an Employee at the YMPE (Scenario B), 1995, 2020, and 2030*

Tax-Indexing Mode (1)	Indices[a]		Share of Earnings		
	Real Disposable Income (2)	Real Income Taxes (4)	Nominal Income Tax Rate (5)	Taxes Plus CPP (6)	Income Taxes Only (7)
	(1995 = 100)		*(%)*	*(%)*	*(%)*
			1995		
	100	100	24.0	25.8	23.3
			2020		
Earnings[b]	122	121	24.0	28.1	22.5
Revenue[c]	120	126	24.9	29.0	23.3
CPI[d]	116	140	27.5	31.6	26.0
CPI-3[e]	102	184	35.7	39.8	34.2
			2030		
Earnings[b]	133	132	24.0	28.6	22.3
Revenue[c]	131	138	25.0	29.6	23.3
CPI[d]	125	160	28.7	33.3	27.0
CPI-3[e]	105	221	38.9	43.5	37.2

[a] Index minus 100 is the real percentage increase from 1995.

[b] Tax brackets and allowances are indexed to earnings growth.

[c] Taxesare kept at the same proportion of earnings as in 1995.

[d] Taxes are indexed to inflation (that is, to the consumer price index).

[e] Taxes are indexed to inflation minus three percentage points.

Note: The table assumes earnings increase by 4.5 percent per annum and inflation is 3.5 percent per annum. Federal marginal tax rates (17 percent, 26 percent, 29 percent) and the federal surtax (3 percent of basic federal tax) do not change over time; provincial taxes are 54.5 percent of basic federal tax.

Source: Dickinson 1995.

point (23.3 percent to 22.5 percent) because the CPP tax credit rises with the contribution rate.

If tax brackets and allowances were indexed to keep income tax revenues the same proportion of earnings as they were in 1995, the effect would be the same as indexing to earnings and disallowing any tax credit on the *increase* in CPP contributions after 1995. Disposable income would increase by 20 percent between 1995 and 2020, and by 31 percent between 1995 and 2030. The real value of tax revenues would increase by 26 percent to 2020 and by 38 percent to 2030.

Obviously, economic growth cannot be treated as a detail or technicality. To illustrate the importance of real growth, alternative projections were made assuming no change in real earnings. These projections (not shown on Table 5) indicate that real disposable income of workers at the YMPE would fall by 3 to 5 percent between 1995 and 2030, depending on how the tax system was indexed.[17] However, income tax revenues likely would be a major problem if increases in the seniors' dependency ratio called for more real tax revenue per person and per worker, not less.

Real growth also reduces the upward pressure on CPP contribution rates because the YMPE is indexed to earnings growth while benefits are indexed to inflation. This difference is a powerful cost-control feature, especially as seniors become a larger share of the population and life expectancy increases. For example, people who retire at age 65 and live to age 85 spend nearly one-third of their adult lives in retirement. During these 20 years, real growth increases the standard of living of contributors but not recipients. The difference disappears when there is no real growth.

Therefore, whatever concerns there might be about future generations' *willingness* to pay the projected increases in CPP contributions, the standard of living should be higher than it is

---

17 Only two tax scenarios are implied here: indexing to earnings (which is the same as indexing to inflation when there is no real growth), and keeping tax revenues a constant share of earnings. With no economic growth, the CPI-3 scenario would be even more unrealistic.

today unless there is a substantial increase in income tax rates. The projections for real disposable income do not suggest that future workers will be less *able* than are current workers to pay CPP contributions.

In my analysis, I use the same rates of inflation and earnings growth as the CPP projections, not only for consistency with the projected contribution rates but also because I do not want to speculate about what the real growth rate will be. Frankly, I have little notion of what the economy and technology will look like 25, 35, or 45 years hence. I leave it to the reader to consider whether people's perceptions and fears would be different if they knew that the real growth rates used to project the increase in CPP contribution rates between 1995 and 2030 could allow the real value of take-home pay to increase by one-quarter to one-third over those 35 years.

> ### Misperception 5: Today's younger workers will earn no interest on their CPP retirement contributions, and future generations will receive less in benefits than they pay in contributions.

Here, the focus shifts from future contributors' *ability* to pay CPP contributions to their *willingness* to invest in CPP pensions. There is a perception that today's younger contributors will be short changed by the CPP. In this view, people born in 1920 and retiring in 1985 will take seven times more out of the CPP than they put in, while those born in 1980 will get a dollar back for each dollar contributed, and those born in 2000 will get back only 80 cents on the dollar (Dalglish 1992). Simply put, the baby boom generation will pass the cost of its retirement on to the baby bust generation.

Cohort Rates of Return

The cohort rate of return is the rate of return on the total employer-plus-employee contributions of all people born in the same year. The annual rate of return is equivalent to the rate of interest that would have to be earned on each dollar contributed by members of the cohort, from the time it is contributed to the time it is paid as a benefit, if the cohort's own contributions were to finance all its own benefits.

Comments in the media leave the impression that nominal rates of return — that is, the rates of return before adjusting for inflation — will be zero or negative: "Someone born in 1980 would see benefits exactly equalling contributions" (Hadekel 1993); and "[t]he next generation is going to be asked to make contributions that will significantly exceed the benefits they can ever hope to receive from the CPP" (Dalglish 1992).

Such statements can be misleading if casually read. Certainly, Table 6 shows that the rates of return on CPP contributions for the earliest contributors were far greater than for later cohorts. Future cohorts will not, however, see negative rates of return. Rates of return were high for early cohorts because contribution rates were low in the earlier years of the plan and because the CPP was phased in over a short period of ten years — which meant that the cohort born in 1922 could retire on a full pension after contributing for only ten years. The chief actuary estimates that the effect on CPP expenditures of this short phase-in period will be negligible soon after 2000.

The cohort rates of return are very much the same for Scenario A, Scenario B, and pay-as-you-go (PAYGO) contribution rates, which justifies using the PAYGO rates in later sections. The cohort PAYGO rates of return are calculated from the annual PAYGO rates, which are the contribution rates that would be needed each year if that year's contributions were to equal the same year's expenditures exactly.[18]

The 1962 cohort, born near the end of the baby boom, gets a nominal rate of return of about 7 percent per annum. Today's

---

18 The annual rates of return in Table 6 are "internal rates of return." There is a unique internal rate of return for each cohort, because CPP participants pay all their contributions *before* they start receiving benefits. In other words, they do not fluctuate back and forth as contributors and beneficiaries.

Table 6:   *Rates of Return on*
             CPP Contributions, by Cohort

Year of Birth	Year Contributions Start	Annual (Nominal) Rates of Return Using:		
		Scenario A	Scenario B	PAYGO
		(%)	*(%)*	*(%)*
1922	1966	19.64	19.64	44.35
1942	1966	11.07	11.02	12.17
1962	1980	7.38	7.11	6.76
1972	1990	6.18	6.04	5.95
1982	2000	5.36	5.40	5.42
1992	2010	4.94	5.10	5.09
2012	2030	4.96	5.03	5.00
2022	2040	5.04	5.06	5.01

Source: Canada, Office of the Superintendent of Financial Institutions.

Notes: Returns for the 2022 cohort are slight underestimates since some years of benefits
         are lost because the model devised by the Office of the Superintendent of Financial
         Institutions predicts to 2100. The structure of CPP contributions and benefits
         satisfies the technical conditions for a unique internal rate of return.

younger workers — say, those who were born in 1972 and entered
the labor force in 1990 — see a nominal rate of return of about
6 percent per annum. Deducting 3.5 percentage points for inflation[19] gives a real rate of return of 2.5 percent per annum. For
people born in and after 1992, cohort rates of return stabilize at
about 5 percent per annum, giving real returns of about 1.5 percent per annum.

Cohort rates of return have created misperceptions because
statistics have been misinterpreted, or at least their implications
have not been explained properly. The statistical method used to
estimate the returns in Table 6 essentially asks the question: At
what rate of interest would the value of all the cohort's contributions equal the value of all it: benefits? An alternative method

19 The chief actuary's projections assume this rate of inflation.

asks the question: How does the value of cohort contributions compare with the value of its benefits, at an *assumed* rate of interest?

When the estimated values of benefits and contributions are equal using the second method, the rate of return equals the assumed rate of interest.[20] Apparently, the values of the 1980 cohort's benefits and contributions would be the same at an assumed interest rate of about 6 percent. This means the rate of return for the 1980 cohort would be 6 percent. It does *not* mean "benefits equal contributions," which implies a zero nominal rate of return and a real rate of *minus* 3.5 percent per annum.

Similarly, a statistic of 0.8 estimated by the second method for the cohort born in 2000 means the value of the cohort's benefits will be four-fifths of the value they would be if contributions were invested at the assumed rate of interest. It does *not* mean the cohort will receive 80 cents per dollar contributed, which is a negative nominal rate of return; rather, it simply means the rate of return is less than the assumed interest rate.

These cohort rates of return have created false perceptions for other reasons, too. For example, my conversations with friends and colleagues suggest that the statements in the press have been taken to mean a zero or negative return on just the *employee's share* of CPP contributions. Moreover, cohort rates of return do not distinguish between the insurance and investment components of CPP benefits and contributions. Individuals surely do not want to maximize their monetary return on disability insurance or life insurance premiums by becoming disabled or dying early!

Pensioners' Rates of Return

This section examines a variety of rates of return for individual contributors born in 1974, 1992, and 2020, as presented in Table 7. The individuals are assumed to receive retirement pensions from the CPP only after retiring at age 65. An individual's lifetime contributions are found by applying each year's CPP contribution

---

20 Technically, the ratio of "present values" equals one.

rate to that same year's contributory earnings for all years. Earnings are assumed to grow at 4.5 percent per year. The initial pension at age 65 is calculated from the history of pensionable earnings and is then increased each year by 3.5 percent to compensate for inflation. The nominal rate of return is calculated from the individual's lifetime history of contributions and benefits, using the same statistical method as in Table 6. The real rate of return is the nominal rate minus 3.5 percentage points for inflation. Income taxes on benefits and the tax credit on contributions are ignored.[21]

The estimates assume that individuals do not contribute for the first seven years of the contributory period, which does not affect the retirement pension since this period is covered by the general dropout provision. Childrearing dropouts are ignored, so the rates of return are underestimates for a large proportion of the population. Rates of return are estimated for three types of workers: the self-employed worker at YMPE pays both the employer and employee shares of contributions, and realizes the lowest possible return; the employee at YMPE receives a higher rate of return because the retirement pension is treated as the return on only the employee share of contributions; for the employee at half the YMPE, the return is higher still, because the pension is half that of the worker at YMPE but contributions are less than half.

For the self-employed contributor at YMPE in all cohorts, the nominal rates of return on all CPP contributions, including the disability and survivor benefit components, are small but positive at age 75, and real rates of return are negative. However, the real rate of return becomes positive at age 80 in the 1974 cohort, and at age 85 in the later cohorts.

Real annual rates of return on the employee's share of contributions at YMPE are positive even at age 75. For the 1974 cohort, the nominal rate of return on the employee's share is

---

21 In fact, the after-tax and before-tax rates of return are the same if the individual is in the 17 percent federal tax bracket during retirement.

Table 7:   *Individual Nominal Rates of Return with Retirement Pension and Investment-Plus-Insurance Contributions, 1974, 1992, and 2020 Cohorts*

Age at Death (1)	Self-Employed: YMPE		Employee: YMPE		Employee: 50% YMPE	
	Scenario B (2)	PAYGO (3)	Scenario B (4)	PAYGO (5)	Scenario B (6)	PAYGO (7)
	(percent)					
	1974 Cohort					
90	5.29	5.28	7.63	7.61	8.02	8.00
85	4.65	4.64	7.17	7.15	7.59	7.57
80	3.64	3.63	6.43	6.41	6.88	6.86
75	1.86	1.84	5.10	5.08	5.61	5.60
	1992 Cohort					
90	4.72	4.71	6.94	6.93	7.31	7.31
85	4.07	4.05	6.46	6.45	6.86	6.85
80	3.05	3.03	5.71	5.69	6.14	6.13
75	1.29	1.26	4.38	4.36	4.87	4.85
	2020 Cohort					
90	4.64	4.60	6.84	6.80	7.21	7.17
85	3.99	3.94	6.36	6.32	6.75	6.71
80	2.98	2.92	5.61	5.56	6.03	5.98
75	1.23	1.15	4.28	4.22	4.77	4.71

Notes: See the text for explanations of PAYGO and Scenario B. Estimates allow for the general dropout of 15 percent of the contributory period. In this table, the dropout is seven years, and the individual contributes for 40 years from age 25. Individuals contributing for the full 47 years would have rates of return about 90 percent of those in the table. There are no childrearing dropout or survivor pensions. Individuals die on the last day of the age/year shown.

almost 6.5 percent per annum at age 80 and over 7 percent at age 85 (column 4). Real rates of return on the employee's share in the 1974 cohort are between 3 percent and 4 percent per annum for retirees in their 80s, but up to one percentage point lower in later cohorts. In all cohorts, the nominal and real rates on the employee's share at half the YMPE exceed those at the YMPE by up to half a percentage point. For example, nominal rates of return approach 7 percent at age 80 in the 1974 cohort and age 85 in later cohorts and real rates of return are almost 3.5 percent at these ages.

Obviously, nominal rates of return are neither zero nor negative. However, the pensioner must live to about age 80 in the 1974 cohort and to age 85 in later cohorts before a positive real rate of return is realized on employer-plus-employee contributions.

Individual Returns to "Investment"

In this section, individuals' pensions are the same as in the previous section, but they are expressed as a return on only the *investment* component of CPP contributions (see Table 8). This approach is consistent with the concept of investment rather than insurance. Viewed in this light, negative real rates of return all but disappear, even for the self-employed worker at YMPE.

Since the survivor benefit component of contributions is part investment and part insurance, each year's PAYGO contributions are divided into the share that finances everything except disability benefits (PAYGO-XD) and the share that finances only retirement pensions (PAYGO-R). Contributions are calculated by applying the PAYGO-XD and PAYGO-R rates to contributory earnings in the same manner as before, and rates of return calculated as if retirement pensions were the only return on these contributions (Table 8).[22]

22 For example, if the retirement pension is 70 percent of all CPP expenditures in a given year, the PAYGO-R contribution rate is 70 percent of the PAYGO-ALL rate.

Table 8: *Individual Nominal Rates of Return with Retirement Pension and "Investment" Shares of Contributions, 1974, 1992, and 2020 Cohorts*

Age at Death (1)	Share of PAYGO, Self-Employed: YMPE			Share of PAYGO, Employee: YMPE			Share of PAYGO, Employee: 50% YMPE		
	Full^a (2)	XD^b (3)	R^c (4)	Full^a (5)	XD^b (6)	R^c (7)	Full^a (8)	XD^b (9)	R^c (10)
				(percent)					
				1974 Cohort					
90	5.28	5.99	6.62	7.61	8.34	8.97	8.00	8.73	9.37
85	4.64	5.40	6.08	7.15	7.92	8.59	7.57	8.33	9.00
80	3.63	4.47	5.20	6.41	7.23	7.95	6.86	7.68	8.39
75	1.84	2.79	3.64	5.08	5.99	6.78	5.60	6.49	7.27
				1992 Cohort					
90	4.71	5.23	5.75	6.93	7.46	7.97	7.31	7.84	8.34
85	4.05	4.62	5.18	6.45	7.02	7.55	6.85	7.41	7.95
80	3.03	3.66	4.28	5.69	6.30	6.88	6.13	6.73	7.30
75	1.26	1.99	2.72	4.36	5.03	5.68	4.85	5.52	6.16
				2020 Cohort					
90	4.60	5.04	5.52	6.80	7.23	7.71	7.17	7.60	8.08
85	3.94	4.41	4.94	6.32	6.78	7.29	6.71	7.17	7.68
80	2.92	3.45	4.03	5.56	6.05	6.61	5.98	6.48	7.03
75	1.15	1.77	2.45	4.22	4.78	5.40	4.71	5.26	5.87

^{a} Same as PAYGO in Table 7; see the text for an explanation.

^{b} Retirement pensions' rate of return to all but the disability benefit share of contributions.

^{c} Return to the retirement pension share of contributions.

Notes: See Table 7.

For the self-employed worker at YMPE, the real annual rate of return at age 80 in the 1974 cohort is nearly 1 percent when the disability insurance component of contributions is omitted (column 3), and 1.7 percent on only the retirement pension component of contributions (column 4). By age 85, the nominal returns are 5.4 percent and 6.08 percent per annum, respectively, giving real returns of approximately 2 percent and 1.5 percent. Real and nominal rates are about one percentage point lower in the 1992 cohort, and slightly more than one percentage point lower in the 2020 cohort.

Even though the real rates of return on the investment components of employer-plus-employee contributions at YMPE may be small, the nominal rates of return are usually much higher than the zero and negative rates gleaned from a casual reading of press reports. The annual rates of return on the employee's share of contributions are higher still. At YMPE in the 1974 cohort, nominal rates on all but the disability insurance component of contributions exceed 7 percent at age 80, and are almost 8 percent at age 85 (column 6). The corresponding real rates of return are 3.73 percent and 4.42 percent per annum. The real rates of return rise to 4.45 percent and 5.09 percent on the retirement pension component of contributions (column 7).

Even in the 2020 cohort, people living into their 80s see nominal rates of return of between 6 and 7 percent on the employee's share of all but the disability component of contributions. In all cohorts, the nominal and real rates of return on the employee's share at half the YMPE is almost half a percentage point higher than at the YMPE. In other words, not only are popular perceptions of cohort rates of return seriously flawed; the rates of return on the employee's share of contributions investment in CPP retirement pensions are generally higher than the cohort rates of return.

When people contribute to the CPP, they are both investing in their retirement and buying insurance. Insurance premiums provide income in the event of circumstances we hope will *not* arise, such as an early death or a severe and prolonged disability. Pension contributions provide income in a circumstance — a lengthy retirement — we surely hope *will* arise. Individuals generally like to plan on the basis of optimistic expectations of their personal longevity, which will affect their perceptions of the rate of return and their overall support for the CPP.

Since perceptions and misperceptions are the main topic of this paper, I must leave three considerations to the reader. First, will most people think that references in the media are to nominal or to real rates of return? Second, will they think that the rates of return they read about are for the amounts they see on their pay cheques and year-end tax returns? Third, what value do contributors attach to the insurance aspects of the CPP and to other attributes, such as the purchasing power of their inflation-protected pensions? And how do these things affect the minimum acceptable monetary rates of return?

Misperception 6: The CPP is approaching bankruptcy, imposing a second national debt on future generations, and creating unacceptably high transfers from Generation X to the aging baby boom generation.

Concerns about the financial and fiscal viability of the CPP compound the negative effect of the misperceptions already discussed. Again, the concerns seem to be exaggerated because of the focus on the projected increases in CPP contribution rates.

Is the CPP
Approaching Bankruptcy?

The CPP is basically a pay-as-you-go plan: after 2010, the difference between projected contribution rates and PAYGO rates is seldom more than half a percentage point. Although the plan cannot go bankrupt in the legal sense, the word is often used in conjunction with references to depletion of the CPP account.

Linking projections of the CPP account to bankruptcy is mislead-ing, to say the least. If the account continues to fall, raising contribution rates in the near future will replenish it and take some of the pressure off contribution rates in the more distant future, as with Scenario B. This is not bankruptcy.

At the end of 1992, the CPP account was worth about 8.5 percent of the total pensions promised to current and future retirees who have contributed and are contributing to the plan. The account is a small proportion of the total liability because the plan was designed that way, not because it is going broke. The role of the account is to help smooth contribution rates over time, to avoid unexpected short-term fluctuations in the contribution rate, and to provide a short term contingency fund to pay benefits if federal-provincial agreements on contribution rates are de-layed. Also, the increase in contribution rates needed to replenish the account depends on whether the recent increase in disability benefit claims is permanent or temporary.

What Is the
"Second National Debt"?

The CPP's unfunded liability is the pension promises already acquired by contributors, minus the amount in the CPP account. At the end of 1992, the CPP account ($42.3 billion) was about 8.5 percent of total pension promises ($496.3 billion), leaving an unfunded liability of about 91.5 percent of the total (Canada 1992). This unfunded liability is being called a "second national debt." To put the unfunded liability in context, in 1992 assets of public and private RPPs and RRSPs were about $416 billion, and PAYGO plans for federal and provincial government employees had unfunded liabilities of $106 billion.

These are huge numbers, but the CPP's unfunded liability should be seen in the proper light. First, unlike the real national debt, the CPP's unfunded liability has yet to be spent. Second, the accounting method used for the CPP is different from that used for other government programs because the CPP is funded from contribution rates, not general revenues. Other government programs, such as the GIS, may also be paying benefits well into the future, but government accounting methods do not ask how much money is needed now to finance such programs for the next 50 years.

To illustrate, I have done a back-of-the-envelope calculation assuming that the basic design of OAS/GIS remains unchanged for the next 40 years. In September 1994, more than 1.37 million seniors (over 40 percent of OAS recipients) received $387.7 million from the GIS, which implies they received another $532 million from OAS, for a total of $919.9 million. If the number of GIS recipients remains unchanged, the unfunded liability of OAS/GIS benefits paid to GIS recipients over the next 40 years is about $250 billion.[23] If the number of GIS recipients were to double by 2033 as the baby boomers retire, the unfunded liability would be about $340 billion — more than half the total (unfunded plus funded) liability of the CPP/QPP ($672 billion).[24] Without CPP/QPP benefits, the $340 billion would increase by one-half of the CPP/QPP benefits that would have been paid to GIS recipients.

A brief comparison with private plans is useful here. Very simply, these plans may not be as fully funded as one assumes, perhaps because contribution rates have not been adjusted for increased longevity. In 1988, for example, Ontario hospitals took a contribution holiday (no longer allowed in Ontario) because the pension fund had an actuarial surplus. A later actuarial survey included other factors that the chief actuary always incorporates into the CPP projections,[25] and discovered that the plan actually had an unfunded liability. Since then, the employee's contribution

---

23 For compatibility with the CPP estimates, the OAS/GIS estimate assumes 2 percent annual inflation to 2000 and 3.5 percent thereafter, and a 6 percent annual interest rate. The discounted present value (that is, the unfunded liability) does not include SPA payments to seniors' spouses aged 60 to 64.

24 Assuming that the number of recipients increases by a constant 1.8 percent per year.

25 For example, the age of members, lower rates of return on investment, separation rates (including early retirement), and increased longevity.

rate has increased by one-third, even though employers paid the accumulated deficiency.

Intergenerational Transfers through the CPP

With respect to intergenerational transfers, some perspective is again needed before looking at the data. First of all, such transfers are not necessarily bad if society accepts that there should be some smoothing of the income distribution. Some intergenerational transfers are also interpersonal transfers, since several generations are alive at the same time. It can also be misleading to take any one program out of its context in the overall system. For example, how much of the CPP's intergenerational transfer to baby boomers will be returned through higher income tax revenues and lower costs of programs such as the GIS? At any point, gross CPP expenditures are less than the plan's net transfers from contributors to recipients (that is, at last-payer values). A close look at Table 9 will help here.

The no-transfer contribution rate (column 2) is the percentage of contributory earnings that a cohort would have to contribute and invest if its own contributions and accumulated interest were to finance its own CPP benefits fully. At this contribution rate, there would be no transfers through the CPP to or from other cohorts. The no-transfer contribution rates assume an interest rate of 6 percent per annum on the contributions that would be invested by each cohort.[26] The difference between the no-transfer rate and the weighted average of PAYGO rates over the cohort's whole contributory period is an indicator of intergenerational transfers through the CPP.

For the 1974 cohort, the no-transfer contribution rate (10.57 percent) is 86 percent of the lifetime PAYGO rate (12.35 percent), as shown in column 3, a difference of 1.78 percentage points.

---

26 Six percent is the rate assumed in the chief actuary's CPP projections.

Table 9: *Lifetime CPP Contribution Rates, 1974 and 2022 Cohorts*

Year of Birth (1)	No-Transfer Rate (2)	Weighted Average PAYGO (3)	PAYGO minus No-Transfer (4)	Retirement-Only Contribution Rates	
				No-Transfer (5)	PAYGO (6)
With Mortality Improvements					
1974	10.57	12.35	1.78	7.45	8.61
2022	10.62	14.34	3.72	8.00	10.83
Without Mortality Improvements					
1974	9.51	11.75	2.24	6.30	7.85
2022	8.99	12.69	3.70	6.28	9.03
Percentage Point Difference					
1974	1.06	0.60	—	1.15	0.76
2022	1.63	1.65	—	1.72	1.80

Source: Canada 1995.

Note: The no-transfer contribution rate is what the cohort would pay to fully fund its own benefits, assuming an annual interest rate of 6 percent. The PAYGO rate is a weighted average of all the PAYGO rates in the contributory period.

Therefore, the lifetime PAYGO rate is only 17 percent higher than the rate that would totally eliminate intergenerational transfers through the CPP. Since a significant share of CPP benefits in any year is returned in taxes and lower costs of other programs, the net intergenerational transfers from the 1974 cohort should be quite small.

This 17 percent difference between the no-transfer rate and the lifetime PAYGO rate contrasts markedly with the increase in CPP contribution rates over time, and likely leaves a very different perception of how much Generation X will transfer to the baby boomers. The CPP contribution rate projected in Scenario B almost triples over the 1974 cohort's contributory period, from 4.8 percent in 1992 to 14 percent in 2058.

There are three reasons why the difference between the two lifetime rates is quite small for the 1974 cohort. First, the very presence of the baby boomers keeps PAYGO rates below the no-transfer rate until 2014, which is more than halfway through the 1974 cohort's contributory period.[27] Second, after 2014, part of the baby boom generation is retired but the other part is still working and contributing. Third, the 1974 cohort's lifetime PAYGO rate does not pay the full cost of the cohort's own increased longevity.[28]

Without the projected improvements in the mortality rate over time and in life expectancy at age 65, the lifetime PAYGO rate (column 3) would fall by less than 5 percent (12.35 percent to 11.75 percent). But the no-transfer rate (column 2) would fall by 10 percent (10.57 percent to 9.51 percent), since the cohort would not have to finance the extra years in retirement resulting from its own increased longevity. This effect is apparent in the difference between the no-transfer and PAYGO rates needed to finance only the retirement pension component of CPP benefits. Without mortality improvements, the PAYGO retirement rate (column 6) would fall by less than one-tenth (8.61 percent to 7.85 percent), but the no-transfer retirement rate (column 5) would fall by more than one-sixth (7.45 percent to 6.3 percent).

The situation is very different for the cohort born in 2022, which enters the labor force in 2039 and turns 65 in 2086. Its no-transfer rate (10.62 percent) is only three-quarters of the lifetime PAYGO rate (14.34 percent). In fact, annual PAYGO rates are more than the no-transfer rate over the 2022 cohort's entire

---

27 The CPP contribution rate stays below the no-transfer rate until 2017 in Scenario A and 2012 in Scenario B.

28 Between 1986 and 2100, projected life expectancy at birth increases by 7.3 years for men and 7.2 years for women. Life expectancy at age 65 is projected to increase by 4.4 years (30 percent) for men and 5.4 years (28 percent) for women.

contributory period. The difference in the effect of improved mortality between the 2022 cohort's two lifetime contribution rates is much less than for the 1974 cohort. The cohort obviously benefits from its own improved mortality, but not financially through the CPP.

Without the baby boomers, the 2022 cohort would benefit because later generations would pay for its increase in longevity and in the number of years it receives CPP pensions. But this effect is substantially overpowered by baby boomers in retirement. The 2022 cohort will be paying the pensions of more baby boomers than the 1974 cohort, and for longer. Also, unlike the 1974 cohort, the 2022 cohort gets no advantage from the lower contribution rates while the baby boomers were working. Intergenerational transfers will take a larger share of the earnings of the 2022 cohort than of the 1974 cohort. However, the real disposable income of the 2022 cohort should still be higher if real earnings increase as projected.

In summary, the analysis of lifetime contribution rates indicates that intergenerational transfers to baby boomers from today's younger workers will be far less than suggested by popular perceptions, because of the latter's own increased longevity and their lower contribution rates while baby boomers are working. Future generations will make most of the transfers to the baby boomers through the CPP. Even so, any implications for policy toward the CPP should recognize the interactions with the rest of the system over time, since lower intergenerational transfers through the CPP will likely mean higher intergenerational transfers through other programs, such as the GIS.

Of course, government has a responsibility to future generations as well as to the current one, and the justifiable and desirable level of transfers is largely an ethical question. Intergenerational transfers are as justifiable as interpersonal transfers in principle, but caution should be exercised in practice because the income and resources of future generations are uncertain.

Concluding Remarks

What I have called popular misperceptions about the Canada Pension Plan distort the current seniors' benefit system and exaggerate legitimate concerns about the future. They distort the current system by ignoring interactions among the various components of the tax and transfer and pension system, and by taking component programs out of the context of their appropriate roles in the system. They exaggerate legitimate concerns about the future by implying unfair comparisons, by misinterpreting statistics, and by ignoring the implications of important assumptions and projections underlying the data.

Public pensions are contingent promises and formulas linking the standard of living of pensioners to the general standard of living (Weldon 1991). Current economic and fiscal pressures may require some restructuring of the seniors' benefit system, but popular misperceptions should not be allowed to justify extreme and irreversible measures. How tolerable and acceptable the pension burden will be depends on real growth in average income compounded over many years, on how long it takes to reduce significantly the share of income paid as interest on the national debt, and on pressures for more spending in other policy areas.

References

Canada. 1989. Department of National Health and Welfare. Canada Pension Plan Advisory Board. *The Level of Pension Awareness in Canada*. Ottawa.

——. 1992a. Office of the Superintendent of Financial Institutions. *Canada Pension Plan Fourteenth Actuarial Report as at 31 December 1991*. Ottawa.

——. 1992b. Department of National Health and Welfare. *Evaluation Report, Old Age Security Program*. Ottawa.

——. 1994. Department of Finance. *Jobs and Growth: Creating a Healthy Fiscal Climate*. Ottawa.

——. 1995. Office of the Superintendent of Financial Institutions. *Canada Pension Plan Fifteenth Actuarial Report as at 31 December 1993*. Ottawa.

Canadian Institute of Actuaries. 1993. *Canadian Retirement Income Social Security Programs: Report of the Task Force on Social Security Financing*. [Toronto?].

Chawla, Raj K. 1991a. "Dependence on Government Transfer Payments, 1971–1989." *Perspectives on Labour and Income* (Statistics Canada). Ottawa. Summer.

——. 1991b. "An Aging Society: Another Viewpoint." *Canadian Social Trends* (Statistics Canada). Ottawa. Spring.

Courchene, Thomas J. 1994. *Social Canada in the Millennium: Reform Imperatives and Restructuring Principles*. The Social Policy Challenge 4. Toronto: C.D.Howe Institute.

Coyne, Andrew. 1994. "Canada's other national debt: the tension in pensions." *Globe and Mail* (Toronto). August 13–17.

Dalglish, Brenda. 1992. "Are Pensions Safe?" *Macleans*, March 2, pp. 24–27.

Dickinson, Paul. 1994. *A Study for the Evaluation of the Canada Pension Plan's Retirement Pension*. Ottawa: Department of Human Resources Development.

——. 1995. *The Canada Pension Plan: Supplementary Analysis Pursuant to the Fifteenth Actuarial Report*. Ottawa: Department of Human Resources Development.

Economic Council of Canada. 1990. *Good Jobs, Bad Jobs: Employment in the Service Economy*. Ottawa: Supply and Services Canada.

Fellegi, Ivan P. 1989. "Can We Afford an Aging Society?" *Canadian Economic Observer* (Statistics Canada). Ottawa. October.

Frenken, Hubert. 1990. "RRSPs: Tax-Assisted retirement Savings." *Perspectives on Labour and Income* (Statistics Canada). Ottawa. Winter.

————. and Karen Maser. 1992. "Employer-Sponsored Pension Plans — Who Is Covered?" *Perspectives on Labour and Income* (Statistics Canada). Ottawa. Winter.

Gallup 1985. *Canadians' Attitudes to Pensions and Pension Reform*. Gallup Poll and Allenvest Group, Department of National Health and Welfare.

Gauthier, Pierre. 1991. "Canada's Seniors." *Canadian Social Trends* (Statistics Canada). Ottawa. Autumn.

Ingerman, Sid, and Robin Rowley. 1993. *Another Look at Tax Losses and Retirement Savings*. Montreal: McGill University, Department of Economics.

Hadekel, Peter. 1993. "Governments must move quickly to fine-tune public pension plans." *Montreal Gazette*, November 12.

OECD. 1988. *Ageing Populations: The Social Policy Implications*. Paris: Organisation for Economic Co-operation and Development.

Ross, David P., Richard E. Shillington, and Clarence Lochhead. 1994. *The Canadian Fact Book on Poverty*. Ottawa: Canadian Council on Social Development.

Sarlo, Christopher. 1992. *Poverty in Canada*. Vancouver: Fraser Institute.

Statistics Canada. 1988. *Pension Plans in Canada, 1986*. Ottawa.

Weitz, Harry. 1992. *The Pension Promise*. [Toronto]: Thompson Canada.

Weldon, J. 1991. "On Social Policies in the Canadian Economy." In A. Fenichel and S. Ingerman, eds., *On the Political Economy of Social Democracy: Selected Papers of J.C. Weldon*. Montreal: McGill-Queen's University Press.

The Contributors

John B. Burbidge obtained his PhD from McGill University in 1974 and has taught Economics at McMaster University since then. He held the Faculty of Social Science Chair at the University of Western Ontario in 1993–94. In the late 1970s, he co-authored a paper for the Economic Council of Canada on how public and private pension plans affect the incentive to work. This paper led to a series of publications on social security and the behavior of wealth-holding and consumption over the life cycle, including recent articles in the *Journal of Labor Economics* and *Empirical Economics* (forthcoming).

James Cutt has been a faculty member in the School of Public Administration at the University of Victoria since 1977. Before that, he was a faculty member in the Department of Economics at York University and Foundation Professor of Administrative Studies at the Australian National University.

Paul Dickinson has worked in the area of social policy for two national governments and a provincial government. For the past ten years, he has been a consultant while teaching part time in the Department of Economics at McGill University.

Newman Lam is a Visiting Professor in the School of Public Administration at the University of Victoria. He specializes in the financial analysis of public policies and management information systems.

Michael J. Prince is the Lansdowne Professor of Social Policy in the Faculty of Human and Social Development at the University of Victoria. From 1978 to 1987, he was a member of the School of Public Administration at Carleton University.

Christopher Ragan is Assistant Professor of Economics at McGill University. He received his Master's degree from Queen's University and then completed his Doctoral studies at the Massachusetts Institute of Technology. His general area of research is in macroeconomic theory and policy; his current areas of interest include unemployment theory and monetary policy. He is the co-author (with Richard Lipsey and Paul Courant) of *Economics* (9th Canadian ed.), to be published by Addison-Wesley in 1997. He is also editor of *World Economic Affairs*.

William B.P. Robson is a Senior Policy Analyst at the C.D. Howe Institute and Canadian Liaison Officer for the British-North American Committee. He specializes in Canadian monetary and fiscal policy and has written and edited numerous Institute publications on government budgets and their economic effects and on the Bank of Canada and inflation. He is a familiar commentator on economic issues in the media.

Members of the
C.D. Howe Institute*

---

* The views expressed in this publication are those of the authors and do not necessarily reflect the opinions of the Institute's members.

Chauvco Resources Ltd.
Ciba-Geigy Canada Ltd.
Citibank Canada
Clairvest Group Inc.
Cogeco inc.
Consoltex Group Inc.
Consumers Gas
Coopers & Lybrand
Dr. Glen H. Copplestone
E. Kendall Cork
William J. Cosgrove
Co-Steel Inc.
Marcel Côté
Pierre Côté
John Crispo
Glen E. Cronkwright
John Crow
Crown Life Insurance Company Limited
Paul R. Curley
Thomas P. d'Aquino
Leo de Bever
W. Ross DeGeer
Catherine Delaney
Deloitte & Touche
Desjardins Ducharme Stein Monast
Robert Després
Deutsche Bank Canada
Iain St. C. Dobson
The Dominion of Canada General
    Insurance Company
DuPont Canada Inc.
The Eaton Foundation and The Eaton
    Group of Companies
Gordon H. Eberts
Edper Group Limited
Emerging Markets Advisors Inc.
The Empire Life Insurance Company
ENSIS Corporation
Ernst & Young
Export Development Corporation
Ronald J. Farano, Q.C.
Fidelity Investments Canada Limited
First Marathon Securities Limited
Aaron M. Fish
John P. Fisher
Fishery Products International Limited

C.J. Michael Flavell, Q.C.
Ford Motor Company of Canada,
    Limited
Formula Growth Limited
L. Yves Fortier, C.C., Q.C.
Four Seasons Hotels Limited
GSW Inc.
Jim Garrow
General Electric Canada Inc.
General Motors of Canada Limited
Joseph F. Gill
Gluskin Sheff + Associates Inc.
Goldman Sachs Canada
Goodman Phillips & Vineberg
Peter Goring
Dr. John A.G. Grant
Dr. Jerry Gray
The Great-West Life Assurance
    Company
Greyhound Lines of Canada
Morton Gross
Le Groupe Canam Manac
Groupe Sobeco Inc.
Dr. Geoffrey E. Hale
H. Anthony Hampson
C.M. Harding Foundation
G.R. Heffernan
Lawrence L. Herman
Hewlett-Packard (Canada) Ltd.
Gordon J. Homer
Honeywell Limited
Hongkong Bank of Canada
The Horsham Corporation
Dezsö Horváth
H. Douglas Hunter
Lou Hyndman, Q.C.
IBM Canada Ltd.
Imasco Limited
Imperial Oil Limited
Inco Limited
Inland Industrial Materials Limited
The Insurance Bureau of Canada
Interprovincial Pipe Line Inc.
Investment Dealers Association of
    Canada
The Investment Funds Institute of
    Canada

Publications in "The Social Policy Challenge"

Already Published

1   Watson, William G., John Richards, and David M. Brown. *The Case for Change: Reinventing the Welfare State* (1994). 134 pp.; $12.95. ISBN 0-88806-336-9.

2   Green, Christopher, et al. *Unemployment Insurance: How to Make It Work* (1994). 200 pp. $14.95. ISBN 0-88806-338-5.

3   Harris, Richard G., et al. *Paying Our Way: The Welfare State in Hard Times* (1994). 138 pp.; $12.95. ISBN 0-88806-340-7.

4   Courchene, Thomas J. *Social Canada in the Millennium: Reform Imperatives and Restructuring Principles* (1994). 368 pp.; $19.95. ISBN 0-88806-355-5.

5   Richards, John, et al. *Helping the Poor: A Qualified Case for "Workfare"* (1995). 206 pp.; $14.95. ISBN 0-88806341-5.

6   Fallis, George, et al. *Home Remedies: Rethinking Canadian Housing Policy* (1995). 244 pp.; $14.95. ISBN 0-88806-353-9.

7   Thomason, Terry, et al. *Chronic Stress: Workers' Compensation in the 1990s* (1995). 178 pp.; $14.95. ISBN 0-88806-357-1.

8   Dooley, Martin D., et al. *Family Matters: New Policies for Divorce, Lone Mothers, and Child Poverty* (1995). 290 pp.; $16.95. ISBN 0-88806-354-7.

9   May, Doug, and Alton Hollett, with Brian Lee Crowley and Lars Osberg. *The Rock in a Hard Place: Atlantic Canada and the UI Trap* (1995). 245 pp.; $14.95. ISBN 0-88806-356-3.

10 Adams, Roy J., Gordon Betcherman, and Beth Bilson, with Roger Phillips and John O'Grady. *Good Jobs, Bad Jobs, No Jobs: Tough Choices for Canadian Labor Law* (1995). 198 pp.; $14.95. ISBN 0-88806-352-0.